D0593829

~The~
UNFINISHED
SOUL

~*The*~

UNFINISHED
SOUL

Happening upon Jesus in the Happenstance of Life

CALVIN MILLER

BROADMAN
&HOLMAN
PUBLISHERS

Nashville, Tennessee

THE UNFINISHED SOUL
Copyright © 2004 by Calvin Miller

ISBN 0-8054-3183-7

Broadman and Holman Publishers
Nashville, Tennessee
www.broadmanholman.com

Dewey Decimal Classification: 230
Subject Heading: Christian Life \ Apologetics \ Jesus Christ

Printed in China
1 2 3 4 07 06 05 04

Dedication

To Barbara

Table of Contents

Section 4: Once upon a Time, Jesus
Parables for Postmoderns

Section 5: Frying Rabbits
Putting Jesus Back into the Calendar

Section 6: X-Rated Muffins
Christ and Sexual Sanity

Section 7: The Lawn Mower Man and the Church Lady
Faith Hits Home

Preface

The following bits and pieces of my life have been collected from many years of journals and small articles once written for newspapers, magazines, or other kinds of publications. These offerings are the over-spillings of both the smallest and the most significant moments of my life. These vignettes are not passive. They represent the emotional tracks of my—sometimes explosive—reactions to the various confrontations of heart which have impacted my life.

Are they defining? Worthy?

I believe so. They are teapots and tempests, potholes in the roadway of my years. But then life is rarely an orderly architecture built from large blocks of time. Rather, it is more often a jumbled blueprint: a collage of little events, a composite of small scrapes and brushes, a day-to-day gathering of our significant collisions with ideas. It was rarely during the long lectures at the university where I learned life's greatest truths. My best education came informally wrapped in band-aids. Scraped knees, nuclear explosions, amoebas in culture, cotton candy, the Empire State Building observatory: all these weird and different items are randomly stacked just as they happened—without framework or category.

Circumstances were always my best professors. They were my motley host of unlikely tutors. These lessons came in the hurried proverbs of friends who passed me in the narrow corridors of my life. The truths most central to my well-being were truths I never sat to learn. Rather, I always collided with them. The counsel that still serves me best in life was counsel that initially came flying at me over sick beds or coffee cups. The most needed lines of our lives are rarely from plays. They are usually tossed at us like casual thunderbolts over someone's shoulder.

Further, the most memorable insights were usually sudden and demanding when first I met them. We rarely notice we're headed the wrong way down a one-way road until we meet the head-on traffic. My best friends were those who halted me at the barricades with a simple warning that I was traveling against the flow. To all of them I am in debt.

But above these seemingly accidental occurrences lies my Calvinistic tendency to believe that nothing is completely accidental. Jesus stands over all of life reminding me that he has ordained the course to take the "happen" out of my happenstance. He stuffs his great purposes in the haphazard, which is always as much a hazard as a happening.

Life is a never finished, finishing school. I have not become all I once wanted to be. This collection of small moments proves I am still under construction. This book holds the blueprints of some old structural trials laid by, the maps of the half-walked alleys I never should have gone down in the first place. These events are the dream-pieces of old erector sets (that have been replaced by Legos and Tinkertoys). Still, with careful reading most of my life can be reassembled. Sure, there are parts missing and packing lists improperly itemized. So don't read this book to see how to do anything. Just sit with me and wonder at how closely our pilgrimages have passed. I have a feeling our journeys have been similar. But even if they are not, true pilgrims always understand each other. All of them know that the pilgrimage will always be the main thing, and that every apparent tumble is a tutor whose lessons are free but never cheap.

Calvin Miller
Samford University
Birmingham, Alabama
2004

The Night the Wind Blew

Pentecost 1966 found me in the Brussels Cathedral of St. Michael. The Holiday Mass offered me an hour of reflection as the high-church worship flew at me in two languages: Latin (which I understood only intermittently) and Flemish (which I understood not at all). Thirty of us were gathered in the front of this great cathedral, which stretched cavernous and dark behind us.

The Eucharist was most medieval and colorful. The office was read by a red-robed cardinal attended by two Swiss guards. With all its officious gallantry and the plumage of the worship leader, the great church seemed to embarrass the little crowd huddled near the altar end of the cathedral. The ghostly echoes of the holy words flew through the vacuous and dank air of the middle-earth temple.

I could tell the unintelligible service was about the Holy Spirit, so I thumbed my English Bible to the second chapter of Acts and tried to keep faith with the cardinal, who was totally unaware that a Baptist from America was there, spying on his litany and very much in need of a word from the Lord. It was Pentecost: a day for celebrating that time when the Spirit first fell upon the church. The wind blew then; the flame danced, too. Indeed, the mitre of the bishop was in the shape of flame as a symbol of the descent of the warm, indwelling God. On this day, in this place, the infilling and overarching presence of the Trinity came slashing across the language barriers to reveal himself to me.

The bishop swung the censer, and the sweet odor of incense drifted from the altar, heady as a drink of new wine. I suddenly understood why the early churches were accused of a giddy and immoderate inebriation. Those whom the Spirit washed were drunk on God. The first disciples were elated, out of touch with their business-for-business world. They danced the streets mad with joy, speaking in languages they'd never learned to foreigners from countries they'd never visited.

The scene from the second chapter of Acts swam in my reverie, calling to mind a rustic Oklahoma tent revival, where I first met the Holy Spirit two decades earlier. I was nine years old when World War II ended. Hiroshima and Nagasaki each sounded a little like Native American tribes, and each had the same number of syllables as Oklahoma. I couldn't imagine exactly where these cities were, but the whole world had come to focus on their desperation. The adults in my world talked of little else. Pictures of these places, under headline letters thick as my young fingers, covered the newspapers black with smudgeable ink. My four brothers-in-law would soon come home, those headlines said. Indeed, we thanked God that the possibility of their dying had passed.

In that very year of joy and cataclysm, the Pentecostals erected a tent. (There was little use in asking where the Pentecostals got their tents. It was like asking where Ringling Brothers got their tents. Pentecostals had tents, that was all!) And they came to our town.

Their big-top tabernacle rose above a swampy, snaky tent site. The tent was wind-billowed as the happy accordion sounds of rural singing filled the canvas like sails. The tent swayed but never fell, for it was held up by ropes staked taut as the guitar strings that played along with the reedy accordions. The tent looked like a huge orange jack-o'-lantern, lit by dangling light-bulbs, around which swarmed the candle-flies of August.

Always with August came revivals, as medicine shows came in June. Both "shows" peddled their wares in canvas cathedrals, floored with wood chips, domed with amber tarpaulins, pewed with two-by-twelve boards resting on concrete blocks.

I found myself seated, shirtless, and shoeless on one of those pew boards. Worst of all, I was not "saved." I knew that, and the Pentecostals suspected it. Indeed they suspected everyone of standing in dire spiritual need.

Oklahoma Pentecostals had divided all the world into two broad categories: saved and unsaved. By the age of nine, I knew which category was mine. But my category was not dire. After all, that's why the Pentecostals had tent revivals—so people could change categories. The Person who helped change the categories was the Holy Spirit. That was what the Spirit did: he helped the lost get saved.

Most of the *dramatis personae* of this rural drama now escape me. I do remember two huge very saved Italians, the Solarno Brothers—or maybe it was the Palermo Brothers or the Corsicano Brothers—who played monstrous John-Deere-sized accordions. There was also an unforgettable reformed drunkard who, through streaming tears, told how he had been set free of the devil's power. One of the athletic evangelists wore a leather buckskin coat, whose swishing, dangling strips of cowhide fringe lured the eye hypnotically as he made the earth tremble with his booming voice.

I listened, sincerely and with fear. Who wouldn't? As Nagasaki yet smoldered, this red-eyed prophet told us of the great whore of Babylon who would fornicate with the

Antichrist till blood flowed to the horses' bridles. I trembled as he warned us to make ready for apocalyptic hordes of frogs and locusts. After that, he said, the Euphrates River would go bone-dry like the Salt Fork (a sun-parched riverbed of northern Oklahoma). Then Gog and Magog would rise up, and the real tribulation would begin to tribulate.

I quailed wide-eyed as the buckskin jacket rippled on the chest of this doomsayer. This matter was serious. The hymns made me as nervous as the preaching, for they were rapturously exultant about death and all the great things that would come once we had all had the good fortune to die.

"Some glad morning when this life is o'er, I'll fly away," said one hymn. Another rhapsodised, "Almost cannot avail; almost is but to fail; sad, sad the bitter wail, almost but lost."

But the song that choked my voice to silence went, "I was sinking deep in sin, far from the peaceful shore, very deeply stained within, sinking to rise no more." Oh, the pain I felt as the hymns and the accordions lamented my childhood fate.

"Throw out the lifeline across the dark wave," they sang. I was in the dark wave. I needed "the lifeline to be saved."

"In nomine Patris, et Filii, et Spiritus Sancti." The cardinal chanted the words that bound the Mass in Brussels to these aimless mental wanderings through my childhood years. While his Latin office rolled by, I wondered if the cardinal had ever heard any of those old tent hymns like "Farther Along" or "I'll Fly Away." His red robe fascinated me, and so did the medieval garb of the beefeaters who stood like altar guards, staring into the long, dark cavern of St. Michael's.

The cardinal's robe swished as he pivoted and Latinated. Suddenly I realized how different his dress was from the buckskins of the evangelists who preached in the Pentecostal tent. We all have our own denominational costumes, I thought.

Suddenly he lifted the cup, genuflected, and spoke again of the *"Spiritus Sanctus."* Somehow, I knew we were brothers. I had the sense that, for him, this dutiful performance was no mere exercise in memorization. He had convinced me, as best as one can convince anyone at such a distance, that he was "saved."

I'm not sure he would have convinced the buckskinned evangelist—or Sister Rose, our Pentecostal pastor. She, too, was at the revival that Shechinah night when Nagasaki burned in the Orient and another fierce fire burned in my heart.

Sister Rose didn't play around at being religious. That night, as she clamped her eyes shut and tilted her head toward the ceiling, it was as though she could see right through her clenched eyelids and the canvas that domed our primitive glory. Tears streamed down her face. I could tell Sister Rose was saved—truly "filled" with the Holy Ghost. Even Sister Rogers said so, and Sister Rogers had the gift of discernment, which meant that she, more than others, felt that she could tell who truly was filled and who wasn't.

I wasn't. Sister Rogers knew that too, of course.

So when they began to sing "O Why Not Tonight?" it seemed an honest question unblemished by the adenoidal alto harmony that always marked our singing of the invitation. "Step forward to the altar, so you'll never have to step into hell," shouted the evangelist above the plaintive singing.

Sister Rose was weeping. Sister Rogers was discerning. The burden was immense. I broke into tears. Emotion burned like fire through the sawdust chips. Hell, dark as a gospel tent in a power outage, gaped like a black hole before me. I stood weeping, naked, foolish, and undone. What would I do if Gog should come to Garfield County? What if Jesus came that very night? It could happen. Who knew when Christ would come!

Lucky for me, they sang an invitation: "O do not let the Word depart and close thine eyes against the light. Poor sinner, harden not your heart; be saved, oh, tonight." I had no choice. I flew to the arms of Jesus! Wonder of wonders, he did all the hymn said he would do: he snatched my feet from the fiery clay and set me on the rock. I changed categories. I was saved.

What happened to me then in Garfield County was described by a cardinal reading from the book of Acts in a Brussels cathedral:

"And suddenly there came a sound from heaven as of a rushing mighty wind, and it filled all the house where they were sitting. And there appeared unto them cloven tongues like as of fire, and it sat upon each of them. And they were all filled with the Holy Ghost, and began to speak with other tongues, as the Spirit gave them utterance."

The Cardinal did not seem nearly as moving to me as Sister Rose once seemed. Still, I felt the years reach out to embrace each other: 1945 and 1966 were one. That's what the Spirit does: he condenses, integrates, and unifies all our years and experiences. Just as the prophet Joel's words, spoken ages before Christ, embraced Peter's ecstatic sermon of A.D. 27, the ages likewise agree with Chrysostom, Augustine, Aquinas, and yes, Sister Rose. All ages, cultures, and churches are made one by the *Spiritus Sanctus*.

Suddenly I understood: Pentecost is not merely a day on the church calendar; it is fire and wind able to blow and burn anytime. And our elation at this, like that of the Jerusalem pilgrims in the book of Acts, must make us appear as though we are at least capable of getting "drunk on God." The Spirit's joy binds the ages.

But Jesus, in the Gospel of John, says the Spirit is not there just to make us giddy about God. He is there to do the work of conversion. The Acts passage on the Spirit ends with a mass conversion of pilgrims. Conversion is always the best work of the Spirit of God.

In my life it was true. I wondered, though, how the cardinal had come to know the Spirit? How diverse must be the ways of God to make an educated cardinal and a bashful child of nine one in Christ. Still, this is his most glorious and unitive work across our wide differences.

But, no matter the circumstance, the Spirit's coming is authentic, whenever and wherever it occurs. The coming of the Spirit to my life may have lacked the grandeur of the priest's conversion. As a child, I merely knelt in the sawdust between two big Pentecostal women in flour-sack dresses, and in he came. This experience is as indelible as what Acts describes as "young men having visions, and old men dreaming dreams, and women preaching the glory of his coming."

While I thought about these things, the cardinal all too abruptly swished away; the Mass was over. But as I walked out of the dark church, the sun drenched the world in sunlight, unifying the world with brightness. The costumes were gone; the congregation was back in the streets. Neon blinked its glitzy enticement from bistro to bistro.

But it didn't entice me. God is brighter than neon. There was a fire loose in the world that made Jerusalem, Oklahoma, and Belgium all one. It wasn't as obvious as I might have liked outside the cathedral. Nevertheless the integrating Spirit was there . . . and would always be.

Who knows where the wind may yet blow? Where the flame may yet surprise us? Such a fire lives in us even when it hides, waiting to burn where the coldness of reason has frozen God out of our lives.

"I must have liberty withal, as large a charter as the wind, to blow on whom I please."
William Shakespeare, *As You Like It*

"And with that he breathed on them and said, 'Receive the Holy Spirit.'"
John 20:22

"But when he, the Spirit of truth, comes, he will guide you into all truth. He will not speak on his own; he will speak only what he hears, and he will tell you what is yet to come."
John 16:13

"Which of you fathers, if your son asks for a fish, will give him a snake instead? Or if he asks for an egg, will give him a scorpion? If you then, though you are evil, know how to give good gifts to your children, how much more will your Father in heaven give the Holy Spirit to those who ask him!"
Luke 11:11-13

"You, however, are controlled not by the sinful nature but by the Spirit, if the Spirit of God lives in you. And if anyone does not have the Spirit of Christ, he does not belong to Christ."
Romans 8:9

Section 1

My Easy Christ
Has Left the Church

*Notes on Christian Loyalty in
a Post-Christian World*

My Easy Christ Has Left the Church

Intermittently across my thirty-five years as a pastor, people were quitting the church over this or that objection. Jesus loved them even as they migrated around suburbia looking for the perfect church. These neurotic nomads caused me to wonder if Jesus ever felt like quitting the church. He must have sat a long spell in Gethsemane thinking it all over, while he waited for Judas and the soldiers.

My easy Christ has left the church.
Who can say why?
Maybe it's because his video-logged apostles all
    read diet books, travel agency brochures
    and Christian fiction thrillers
    on how the world should end.
But none read books on what the starving ignorant
    should do until it does.
He left the church so disappointed that Americans
    could all spell "user-friendly"
    but none of them could spell Gethsemane

Can we say for sure he's quit?
Oh yes, it's definite, I'm afraid:
He's canceled his pledge card.
I passed him on the way out of the recreation building
    near the incinerator where we burn
    the leftover religious quarterlies

and the stained paper doilies
from our valentine banquets.
"Quo vadis, Domine?" I asked him.
"Somewhere else," he said.

My easy Christ has left the church,
    walking out of town past seminaries where
    student scholars could all parse the ancient verbs
    but few of them were sure why they had learned the art.
He shook his head confounded that many
    had studied all his ancient words
    without much caring why he said them.
He seemed confused that so many
    studied to be smart, but so few prayed to be holy.

Some say he left the church
    because the part-time missionaries were mostly tourists
    on short-term camera safaris,
    photographing destitution to show the
    pictures to their missionary clubs back home.
I cannot say what all his motives were.
I only know I saw him rummaging through dumpsters
    in Djakarta looking for a scrap of bread
    that he could multiply.
"Quo vadis, Domine?" I asked him.
"Somewhere else," he said.

He's gone—the melancholy Messiah's gone.
I saw him passing by the beltway mega-temple
    circled by its multi-acred asphalt lawn,
    blanketed with imports and huge fat vehicles

nourished on the hydrocarbons of distant oil fields
where the poor dry rice on public roads
and die without a requiem, in unmarked graves.

Is it certain he is gone?

It is.

We saw him in the slums of Recife,
    telling stories of old fools
    who kept on building bigger barns,
    oddly idealistic tales of widows with small coins
    who outgave the richer deacons of the church.

I saw him sitting alone in a fast-food franchise,
    drinking only bottled water and sorting through
    a stack of world-hunger posters.
He couldn't stay long.
He was on the way to sell his
    old books on Calvin and
    Armenius to buy a bag of rice for Bangladesh.

My easy Christ has left the church.
I remember now where I last saw him.
He was sitting in one of those new
    square, crossless mega-churches
    singing 2x choruses and playing bongos
    amid the music stands and amplifiers
    with anonymous Larry and Sherrie.
He turned to them in church and said,
    "I am He, follow me!"

But they told him not to be so confrontational
    and reminded him that they
    had only come for the music and the drama,
    and frankly were offended that he would dare
    to talk to them out loud in church.
After all, they were only seekers, with a right to privacy.

I followed him out through the seven-acre vestibule,
    where he passed the tape-duplicating machine
    where people could buy the "how to" sermons
    of the world's most famous lecturers.

He left the church and threaded his way
    across the crowded parking lot,
    laying down those whips and cords
    he'd once used to cleanse the temple,
    and looked as though he wanted to make
    key-scrapes on Lexi and huge white Audis
    and family buses filled with infant seats.

He stooped and shed a tear after
    and wrote "Ichabod" in the sand.
In a sudden moment I was face to face with him.
"Quo vadis, Domine?" I asked.
"Somewhere else," he said.

My easy Christ has left the church,
    abandoning his all-star role in Easter pageants
    to live incognito in a patchwork culture,
    weeping for all those people who
    can't afford the pageant tickets.

He picked up an old junk cross,
    lugging it into the bookstore
    after the great religious rally,
    and stood dumbfounded
    among the towering stacks of books
    on how to grow a church.
"Are you conservative or liberal," I asked him.
But he only mumbled, "Oh Jerusalem . . ."
    and said the oddest thing about a hen
    gathering her vicious, selfish chicks under her wings.
He left the room as I yelled out after him,
    "Lord, is it true you've quit the church?
    Quo vadis, Domine?"
"Somewhere else," he said.

"We believe that the first time we're born, as children, it's human life given to us; and when we accept Jesus as our Savior, it's a new life. That's what 'born again' means."
Jimmy Carter, interview with Robert L. Turner, March 16, 1976

"Woe to you, teachers of the law and Pharisees, you hypocrites! You are like whitewashed tombs, which look beautiful on the outside but on the inside are full of dead men's bones and everything unclean. In the same way, on the outside you appear to people as righteous but on the inside you are full of hypocrisy and wickedness."
Matthew 23:27-28

"He is the head of the body, the church; he is the beginning and the firstborn from among the dead, so that in everything he might have the supremacy."
Colossians 1:18

The Eighth Deadly Sin

I have always wondered what C. S. Lewis would have had Wormwood say to his charge had his client been a preacher instead of a disgusting demon. Preachers and demons are not the same, but the latter have sometimes mentored the former.

My Dear Rev. Wormwood:

I do not need to remind you that the old list of seven deadly sins has proven fatal to many preachers. They are not all that deadly, however. In fact, when sinned in moderation, they can often be friendly to church growth.

Take envy, for instance. This sin is often the very essence of church growth. Many churches have exploded in size simply because a pastor got a little green-eyed about what a competitor was doing with Christ-centered dance classes or tanning tables. Envy can spark healthy competition. After all, successful pastors serving in the same town often refuse to get really acquainted. Once you really know someone, it's hard to be a ruthless competitor. Let's face it, envy is just plain faster at church growth than charity.

Pride is also quite usable, though it needs to be veneered with false humility. Real humility has never been of much use in church growth. It simply takes too much time. Further, real humility can only be acquired by humiliation, and who needs that?

Gluttony is a must. It is the essential sin of real church growth. Churches move forward on sauces and sweets. When the program is right, you will find few skinny souls. The growing church feeds and eats. For you, however, the trick is not to get too fat. The church likes thin ministers who appear to eat a lot.

Lust is unavoidable, but some ministers have gone too far with it. Still, it's a glandular and somewhat enjoyable sin. Just keep it to yourself and try to look godly while you do it.

Well, I won't tire you with this glum rehearsal of all the deadly sins. But the really important sin for the successful pastor is this: You simply must sin the eighth deadly sin—*the sin of keeping up appearances.*

Sinning this sin is the only way not to be accused of the first seven. It is indeed an answer to them. Whatever sin you sin, keep up the appearance of real righteousness. When you feel proud, look humble. If you must lust, look chaste while you do it. When you are caught up in envy, congratulate the contemporary-worship pastor across town. You don't really have to like other, more-successful pastors; just compliment them. But remember, hypocrisy is a hard art. Watch C-SPAN until you get it down.

Gluttony is a little harder to master. At big, must-do dinners, say loudly, "I'll have my dressing on the side!" Then when the salad really comes, you can quietly dump the dressing all over the top. If the menu is fried chicken at Wednesday night suppers, say loudly, "All the fat is in the skin. I always tear it off." Tear off the skin and lay it temporarily to one side. Then take little bites of the skinned part while you look like the whole chore of eating is interrupting your quiet time. Then take the skin home in your napkin, microwave it for forty seconds on the defrost setting so as not to toughen it, and presto, you can eat the skin and keep your testimony.

Let them see that you are a true minister of Christ. Carry your *Left Behind* Sky Chart into every Spiritual Formation class. Obviously you must own a car of some sort, but shop autos with your spiritual reputation in mind. Toyotas will make you look sincere. And if you must buy a van, it should be a no-frills, maroon Dodge Caravan (two years old) for taking shut-ins to cash their Social Security checks. I know a preacher who bought a new red Taurus and lost his testimony between board meetings. It can happen just that fast. Once the criticism began, he could find no way to shut it down, even by buying a larger "deeper life" notebook. He would have lost his church if he hadn't sold the Taurus and held a week-long seminar on godly spending. Let's face it: there's no way to buy red things and look like the Big Guy.

Also learn to say sanctimonious things. Like if an honest deacon asks if you saw the last episode of *The Sopranos*, say, "No, that's the only time of day I can work in my *Experiencing God* notebook." This will do two things. It will make your deacon feel like a heathen, and it will cause those who overhear your remark to look at you like you are the president of Essenes International.

Remember, everything counts. Never let down your guard. The little things mean a lot.

Read Updike, but keep second-coming novels on your desk. There is no better way to get people to pay less attention to the significance of Jesus' first coming than to embroil them in theories about his second.

Never say "I'm going out to play nine holes!" Say instead, "There's a duffer I need to lead to the Lord. I'll be gone a couple of hours."

Always say, "I am a person of utmost discretion," just before you repeat what you heard in the counseling room. If you're going to preach someone else's sermon, say, "I am indebted to Max Lucado for my opening illustration." Then use his whole sermon. Who's to know?

Consider the little niceties that really count:

"Mrs. Jones, I went by to see your husband in the hospital, but he was asleep."

"I tried to get you on the phone this week. Were you out of town?"

"Have you read the new Deeper Life monographs by Image Press?"

"I found a thrilling insight in Leviticus 19 this week. It has revolutionized my prayer life."

You don't have to actually have done any of these things, but they make lovely conversation starters.

The key is to imply, imply, imply. Project, project, project! Don't be too hard on your purpose-driven smile. Accept your phoniness as a method of church growth. After all, there are very few genuine ministers, and those who *are* genuine are often found in small churches. Who needs that?

Further, those who try to be genuine are in for a lot of work. The best course is to dress like a cable evangelist while you feed your pension fund. In twenty years or so, you can drive a red car and winter in Biloxi. In the meantime get out there and "Practice the Presence of the Big Guy." You don't have to actually *own* his presence; just practice it. Not too rigorously. Get yourself a little "me-time" now and then.

Your devoted uncle,
Screwtape

"Beware, as long as you live, of judging people by appearances."
Jean de La Fontaine, *Fables*

"These are the words of him who holds the seven spirits of God and the seven stars. I know your deeds; you have a reputation of being alive, but you are dead. Wake up! Strengthen what remains and is about to die, for I have not found your deeds complete in the sight of my God. Remember, therefore, what you have received and heard; obey it, and repent. But if you do not wake up, I will come like a thief, and you will not know at what time I will come to you. Yet you have a few people in Sardis who have not soiled their clothes. They will walk with me, dressed in white, for they are worthy. He who overcomes will, like them, be dressed in white. I will never blot out his name from the book of life, but will acknowledge his name before my Father and his angels."
Revelation 3:1-5

"We are not trying to commend ourselves to you again, but are giving you an opportunity to take pride in us, so that you can answer those who take pride in what is seen rather than in what is in the heart."
2 Corinthians 5:12

Good-bye Jesus, from the Media

We are evermore a post-Christian culture. Under the guise of playing fair, the media has isolated the faithful by inundating Christ in secular affairs. In the name of politically correct objectivity, they have excluded the Divine pivot around which Western culture spins.

Dear Jesus,

Good-bye.

We feel a little sheepish writing you,
    what with your being the Son of God and all,
    but we're doing our best to keep from looking
    schmaltzy and corny in New York and Washington.
We are professionals,
    and we must be as dot.com as possible
    in keeping up with our obligations to be sure that
    we do not play favorites in matters of faith.
Buddha and you are roughly equivalent in our view.
That's why we do things the way we do.

This is why
    we don't talk about you much in the papers
    nor cut you any prime-time slack
    in the world of television.

You can imagine what would happen if we
    called you the Son of God
    right on the five o'clock news.
Imagine how the Dalai Lama would feel.
Dropping you out of the five o'clock news
    is all a part of our need to be objective.

It gets a little tough at times, like September 11.
Everybody was noticeably religious for a while.
Even a few Democrats were talking
    non-stop about you then.
But we didn't waver; we just don't do that.
If it helps any,
    we don't do it for Confucius or Zarathustra either.
Secular is best: it just fits us!
God may or may not be there—
    we really don't care.
We are the makers of opinion,
    and in our opinion,
        God only complicates opinion.

We know you said he was your Father,
    but is that really fair?
If he is your Father,
    he can hardly be the Father
    of all these other guys—
    Mohammed, Buddha,
    and the like. . . .
So we are inclined to be objective.
God is nobody's Father—
    or mother, for that matter.

We're not saying God is dead;
    just irrelevant.
We made the decision years ago
    to give you no space in our scheme of things;
    unless, of course, we were doing a story on you
    and how you could not possibly be the kind of
    Messiah the world thinks you are.
We're only doing this to be objective.

After all, there are a lot of people
    who don't believe in you.
This is true of most of us in the media,
    as well as those in Hollywood
    and scads of New England Democrats.
Sure, it's clear—even to us—
    that you've impacted history,
    but then so did Charlemagne and Genghis Khan.
Not that we're comparing you to them.
If you discount the Inquisition and the Crusades,
    your influence was generally more positive than theirs.

But, of course, the biggest part of our ignoring you
    comes from our plain old professional allegiance
    to unbiased reporting.
We don't want to look too Christian.
We'd feel phony!
After all, ninety percent of us have never
    entered a church, unless it's to photograph
    politicians coming out of church.
But then the politicians *should* go to church.
They need it.

They sin a lot, and we need to be there when they do
    to point it out to them.
Plus politicians are running for office—
    it keeps them singing hymns and listening to sermons.
But our jobs are secure,
    so we have no real need to bring you up.

It's hard to retain our objectivity.
We can't bleep you out of every news spot.
Take Mother Theresa during the Clinton presidency.
She spoke of God right during the prayer breakfast.
We cracked a camera lens on that one.
Still, we felt we should let her political incorrectness pass.
What were we to do with a Nobel Laureate who loves Jesus?
    Sheesh!
Our hands were tied.
One time, George Bush also used the word "Jesus,"
    and we left it in,
    mostly because we couldn't think
    of a decent way to bleep it out
    without appearing to be both atheistic and democrat.

9-11 was a tough time for us!
There was Billy Graham talking about you
    right at the National Cathedral.
Humiliating! Running on the way he did!
He just kept it up, talking on and on about you.
Horribly embarrassing, but we learned a long time ago
    that if you try to take the word "Jesus"
    out of everything Graham says,
    he still just stands there reeking charisma.

If he hadn't talked so much about you,
    he might have been a good anchorman.
Too bad we lost him for the best cause!

But all in all, we're winning.
The more we ignore you,
    the less seriously the culture takes you.

So good-bye, Jesus.
Those who need you can take a cathedral tour
    or read some old books.
But don't tune us in at 5:30 p.m.
    hoping to hear your name.
It "ain't-a-gonna" happen.
We're committed to what's-happening-now.
And don't tell us how uncomfortable
    we're going to feel at your second coming.
Even if you do show up next Tuesday,
    we'll bring the world complete coverage on Wednesday.

                    Yours for a myth-free tomorrow,
                    The Media

"From all blindness of heart, from pride, vain-glory, and hypocrisy; from envy, hatred, and malice, and all uncharitableness, Good Lord, deliver us." Litany from the *Book of Common Prayer*

"He went on to say, 'This is why I told you that no one can come to me unless the Father has enabled him.' From this time many of his disciples turned back and no longer followed him. 'You do not want to leave too, do you?' Jesus asked the Twelve. Simon Peter answered him, 'Lord, to whom shall we go? You have the words of eternal life.'" *John 6:65-68*

"Furthermore, since they did not think it worthwhile to retain the knowledge of God, he gave them over to a depraved mind, to do what ought not to be done. They have become filled with every kind of wickedness, evil, greed and depravity. They are full of envy, murder, strife, deceit and malice. They are gossips, slanderers, God-haters, insolent, arrogant and boastful." *Romans 1:28-30*

Dawdling Toward Gomorrah

Gerard Manley Hopkins wrote:
The World is charged with the grandeur of God.
It will flame out, like shining shook from foil;
It gathers to a greatness, like the ooze of oil
Crushed . . . from God's grandeur.

Hear the counsel of God for the last days of Gomorrah:
Fear not I have redeemed you, I have summoned
you by the name; you are mine. (Isa. 43:1)

Several years ago, Robert Bork suggested that we were *Slouching Toward Gomorrah*. Somehow I wish it were possible to ask the Gomorraheans how they felt about Bork's title. My suspicions are that they would resent the title, preferring the title *Slouching Toward Chicago*, or, God forbid, *Slouching Toward Hollywood*.

I don't mean to be crass, but Gomorrah is probably us. I used to think that there was a big sign outside Gomorrah that read, "The Most Wicked City in the World! Depraved is US!" But having observed the human tendency toward self-congratulation, I now believe that the Gomorraheans—as they saw themselves—were very normal and pretty moral.

I have known only a few truly wicked people—and none who really believed they were wicked. Most wicked people see themselves as moral, live-and-let-live people. In Gomorrah, business was booming—the economy was strong. The Gomorrah stock exchange had the Hittites moaning that their own market was in a slump. Plays were rated to keep them safe for the children. The homeless were a constant urban focus. Spear-control was a constant concern. All minorities—even sexual preference minorities, as neighboring Sodom could attest—were protected and cherished. There was no glass ceiling in either commerce or industry. All pride organizations were proud.

It was on a particular Thursday morning after Abraham had laid down his morning newspaper that some angels showed up and surprised him by saying that God was going to rain down burning sulfur and brimstone on the urban show-places.

"Whatever for?" asked Abraham. "Gomorrah is thirty-nine percent born again, and sixty-four percent of the Gomorrahese attend the church or synagogue of their choice at least once a month."

"Yes," said the Lord, "but the culture is wicked."

"Wicked? You mean wicked like the Witch of the East in the Land of Oz?"

"Yes," said the Lord, "Except that Gomorrah is not in Kansas, Toto. Hence, brimstone!"

"But what if there are fifty righteous? Will you spare the city?" After the Lord doubled up in laughter, Abraham knew it was a bad question. Still, to be fair, the Lord agreed that if there were fifty righteous in Gomorrah, he would indeed spare the city.

Then God and Abraham played the famous numbers game of Genesis 18. It was a game that Abraham was prepared to lose, but it called to his mind that he had a nephew living in the other twin city—the one not Gomorrah—and his nephew really liked city living. In fact, his nephew had told him many times that he would rather live there than out in the country with his Uncle Abraham, who just didn't understand the advantages of urban living.

Gomorrah and its sister city at the end of this tale go up in burning sulfur in a single day. But I believe that sometimes brimstone is gradual. Which of Toynbee's twenty-eight civilizations, rotting from within, woke up and suddenly said, "Whoa! Look at us! We're post-modern!" None. Neither did Gomorrah. With civilizations, it is always the case of the amphibian in the stewpot. The only way you can cook one is gradually. So when the brimstone fell on Gomorrah, Abraham and God were bargaining over eroded values in a culture which—as the culture itself saw it—no longer sinned. God's narrow view of things surprised everyone on *Nightline*.

The odd thing is that the people in Gomorrah seemed not to have been aware that God was bargaining with Abraham over the death of their culture. But we who follow Christ should be ever aware that God has a requirement of those who haggle over just how many are righteous in any city. His requirement is that we, like Abraham, are responsible for doing our part in Christ's rescue operation.

Imagine this: God loves Sodom and Gomorrah! The moment we forget that, it is not just Gomorrah that is dead. We, too, are dead. God holds no glee over the death of cultures. He grieves over urban evil and longs to call sinners back to their lost Edens.

It's no easy job being God! To stand for holiness and yet love the unholy is almighty stress—if not for God, for us. To live in Gomorrah and love it is our calling. But to live in Gomorrah and accept it is to accustom ourselves to gradual brimstone.

"Wickedness is always easier than virtue;
for it takes the short cut to everything."
Samuel Johnson, *Journal of a Tour to the Hebrides*

"Woe to you, Korazin! Woe to you, Bethsaida! If the miracles that were performed in you had been performed in Tyre and Sidon, they would have repented long ago in sackcloth and ashes. But I tell you, it will be more bearable for Tyre and Sidon on the day of judgment than for you. And you, Capernaum, will you be lifted up to the skies? No, you will go down to the depths. If the miracles that were performed in you had been performed in Sodom, it would have remained to this day. But I tell you that it will be more bearable for Sodom on the day of judgment than for you."
Matthew 11:21-24

"In a similar way, Sodom and Gomorrah and the surrounding towns gave themselves up to sexual immorality and perversion. They serve as an example to those who suffer the punishment of eternal fire. In the very same way, these dreamers pollute their own bodies, reject authority and slander celestial beings."
Jude 7-8

The Politically Correct Version (PCV) John 7:53-8:12

A plea for biblical simplicity.

John 7:53

(KJV)   And every man went unto his own house.

(PCV)   And everyone, both minorities and social determiners, went to his or her own house in the typically socio-structured city of Jerusalem.

John 8:1

(KJV)   Jesus went unto the mount of Olives.

(PCV)   But Jesus went up to the Mount of Olives. He did not do this to try to be "above" others topographically, but because the population density on the mountain was less environmentally confining, affording him a more meditative matrix for his ego integration.

John 8:2

(KJV)   And early in the morning he came again into the temple, and all the people came unto him; and he sat down, and taught them.

(PCV)   Now, early in the morning—but still well within the hours of fair employment practices—Jesus came again to the temple of Jehovah (not expressing his Jewishness in an arrogant religious exclusivism that would condemn others who called the universal Spirit by their own equally meaningful names). And he (in this instance "he" is not a pronoun of sexual superiority but mere gender identification, because neuterizing the nominative would be confusing) sat down and taught them.

John 8:3

(KJV) And the Scribes and Pharisees brought unto him a woman taken in adultery; and when they had set her in the midst,

(PCV) Then certain religious potentates of the masculine-structured society brought him an oppressed member of the gender-challenged who had been caught in the act of her rightful lifestyle employment. She was shoved to Jesus' feet in an act of religious brutality and, without any bodily covering, was in a state of enforced fabric denial.

John 8:4

(KJV) They said unto him, Master, this woman was taken in adultery, in the very act.

(PCV) They said to him, as opposed to "her" (see parenthetical note on verse 2) "Rabbi, this psycho-sexual, gender-oppressed person was caught performing her unlawful but preferential lifestyle employment."

John 8:5

(KJV) Now Moses in the law commanded us, that such should be stoned: but what sayest thou?

(PCV) "Now Moses, our D.S.S.M. (Dead, Semitic, Sinaitic Male) leader said in the coercive Torah-compulsories that spun off the Ten Behavioral Restrictives, that she should be stoned. What do you say?"

John 8:6

(KJV)   This they said, tempting him, that they might have to accuse him. But Jesus stooped down, and with his finger wrote on the ground, as though he heard them not.

(PCV)   This they said to him, as opposed to her, stressing him with interrogatives. They wanted to prove him guilty of doctrinal aberrations. They wanted to label him as a sexual discriminate. They wanted to display his unfair tendency to look down on people with sexual, ethical, lifestyle differences. Then they would be able to bring their own personal, critical, male establishmentarianism fully against his differing prejudices. But Jesus stooped down and wrote on the ground with his finger. They found it somewhat refreshing that he did not use his finger to point at them in socio-communal separation. Still they found it altogether baffling that he wrote his message in the soft earth. We are not told what the message was.

John 8:7

(KJV)   So when they continued asking him, he lifted up himself, and said unto them, He that is without sin among you, let him first cast a stone at her.

(PCV)   But when they continued questioning him, as opposed to her, he raised himself up, not to indicate any feelings of class superiority but merely to be better heard and said, "Let him or her who is without socially conditioned prejudices among you, first cast a stone at this person." He knew that, reprehensible or not, most people had committed some of these acts and had not worked their feelings out in support groups.

John 8:8

(KJV)   And again he stooped down, and wrote on the ground.

(PCV)   Again he stooped down and wrote on the ground.

John 8:9

(KJV)   And they which heard it, being convicted by their own conscience, went out one by one, beginning at the eldest, even unto the last: and Jesus was left alone, and the woman standing in the midst.

(PCV)   Then those who heard this person were convicted by their own occasional lapses into acts of bad moral conditioning. They began to slip quietly away as though they suddenly remembered what their specific act of unacceptable conditioning was. The oldest left first, since they had more of a backlog of such conditioning. They actually appeared guilty, though none of them said it, because the word "guilty" was an evidence of self-recrimination.

John 8:10

(KJV)   When Jesus had lifted up himself, and saw none but the woman, he said unto her, Woman, where are those thine accusers? hath no man condemned thee?

(PCV)   Finally they were all gone, and Jesus said to the gender oppressed female person, "Gender Oppressed Person, where are your accusers? Have none of the male dominated religious establishment been able to sublimate their self-repression long enough to stone you?"

John 8:11

(KJV) She said, No man, Lord. And Jesus said unto her, Neither do I condemn thee: go and sin no more.

(PCV) "No one, Lord!" she said, wishing she would not have used the word "Lord." She meant it not as a terrible pre-feudal term of masculine empowerment. It was just how she felt at the time. But Jesus said to her, "Neither do I condemn you. Go, but beware of going right back into your preferential lifestyle. It's not just that your preferential employment is somewhat unacceptable to others. This kind of thing can be damaging to your own sense of ego integration."

"Political language . . . is designed to make lies sound truthful and murder respectable, and to give an appearance of solidity to pure wind."
George Orwell, *Politics and the English Language*

"Simply let your 'Yes' by 'Yes,' and your 'No,' 'No'; anything beyond this comes from the evil one."
Matthew 5:37

"So it is with you. Unless you speak intelligible words with your tongue, how will anyone know what you are saying? You will just be speaking into the air."
1 Corinthians 14:9

The Brain

Minds and brains are not the same thing. All of us know plenty of people who have the latter but not the former. The brain is the vehicle of our obedience; the mind is the driver. These fourteen lines came to me after an encounter with a verse of Scripture: "Let this mind be in you which was also in Christ Jesus."

Gray-wrinkled, three-pound thing, I clearly see
I cannot trap you with an EEG.
You nervy organ, you! Skull-cased but free—
A brazen challenge to psychiatry.
Soft mass, I cannot help resenting you
Each time they search and probe for my I.Q.
Half of Einstein's lobe was twice of you,
You joyless mega-volt, computer shoe.

Be careful, Judas organ, or you'll find
God cauterizes every rebel mind.
You small gray lump, you always seethe and grind,
Spend small electric currents thinking blind.

Yet you're the only shabby place I see
That His great mind may come to dwell in me.

"More brain, O Lord, more brain! Or we shall mar utterly
this fair garden we might win."
George Meredith, *Modern Love*

"Your attitude should be the same as that of Christ Jesus."
Philippians 2:5

"The eye is the lamp of the body."
Matthew 6:22

Section 2

On Trapping Werewolves

*Trekking the Full Moon to
the Heart of Hypocrisy*

On Trapping Werewolves

Religious hypocrisy is the worst sort. Who can endure the intolerance of the intolerant? Who would not wish to snub snobs? Yet all intolerance that ends in hate is an offence in heaven.

At the turn of the seventeenth century, a densely wooded section of Transylvania was inhabited largely by Baptists and Lutherans who were both very passionate about God but never cared much for each other. The Baptists were largely trappers, while the Lutherans made cuckoo clocks and nut-crackers.

One day a poor Baptist trapper named Harold was out running his traps just before dawn. "Oh, Lord," he prayed, "I must have a pelt or two to sell at market. Please, Lord, my vife and I are poor, and if the traps are empty again this month, how vill Drusilla"—for that was the name of his wife—"and I eat?"

It was a fair question. God smiled down, and even as Harold prayed, he heard one of his traps snap shut and heard the poor animal baying at the full moon. He knew he had caught a wolf. He plowed through a dense thicket and found the trap which held the howling beast.

The wolf looked at him with pleading eyes. Its leg was badly cut and bleeding from the steel jaws of the trap. Still, its leg was unbroken. Harold took out a long steel blade with which to kill the animal, but the wolf's almost human eyes seemed to say, "Please, no!" Harold sat down and watched while the moon sank beneath the horizon and the sun began to splash color into the first light of day. The wolf suddenly looked mangy and then his fur began to recede. His ears rounded and settled in close to his face. His canine fangs retired into a handsome, human mouth. His eyes squared their slits and his brutish brow became a pompadour haircut. He was staring face-to-face with a real man whose wounded leg, elegantly trousered, was still caught in the trap.

"Hello, I'm Martin!" said the poor, trapped man.

"Dear Gott," said Harold, looking up into heaven, "I ask you for an animal and get a verevolf." Then looking at Martin he said, "I'll bet you're also a Lutheran!"

"Vell, yes, tank Gott I am," said Martin. "How did you know?"

"Most verevolves who show up in my traps turn out to be Lutherans," said Harold.

"You must be a Baptist," said Martin.

"Yes, as a matter of fact I am. How did you know?" asked Harold.

"Most Baptists generalize, critically labeling others," said Martin.

Harold was miffed. "Not only are most verevolves Lutherans, but most Lutherans are arrogant. Almost every time you find an arrogant Lutheran, beneath his lederhosen and wool socks you'll see the scars he's suffered in the traps. I think I'll skin you later and sell you to an Episcopal furrier who lives just south of the old Frankenstein place."

"No, please, let me go!" cried Martin. "Please! Please! Please . . ."

While Martin pled to be free, Harold turned cruelly on his heels and walked off muttering, "Lutherans and verevolves . . . they're all the same. Not vorth a beer and a bratwurst." On his way out of the forest, Harold scratched his hand on a thorn-bush. It bled a bit but presently scabbed into a tiny trickle of blood, which he at first ignored.

"Gutentag, mein Herr!" said Drusilla as he entered their house. "Did you catch anything?"

"Another Lutheran verevolf," said Harold. "No use bringing him back now. Skin a Lutheran and you never get a pelt, only a poorly tailored, cheap suit. But it is still a full moon, so I'll vait till tonight when he is a volf again, and then I'll skin him."

"Ach! Himmel! Vaht is der matter mitt your hand?" Harold looked down. The little cut of the thornbush had caused his hand to swell significantly in size. Worse than that, it had begun to grow long claws and was nearly entirely covered with fur.

"Only von ting can cause dat, mein Herr . . . volfbane."

A chill passed through Harold's Baptist frame.

By noon, hair was growing over Harold's entire body, and at nightfall he disappeared. The only thing Drusilla found were huge paw prints, running from the stoop of their modest home toward the forest. Harold roamed around the entire night, coming home only after the first light of day.

"Harold, mein strudel," asked Drusilla, "are you a volf?"

"Sometimes, part-time, when the moon is full," Harold said sheepishly.

"Harold, I vill not live mitt a volf, even a part-time volf!" shouted Drusilla. "Besides, vaht vill ve tell our friends down at the Baptist church? Do you think they vill let you votch the kinder-tots in the nursery like before? I vant a divorce!"

Harold took a sack of bread and Wiener schnitzel and went back into the woods. He followed the same little shady trail until at last he found Martin. Now Martin was nearly dead with hunger. He gave him the bread and schnitzel and a large cup of wine, and sprang the trap off Martin's swollen leg.

"Martin . . . I'm a volf," Harold said, looking down, ashamed.

"Ah, Harold, I understand, poor soul!"

"I'll never get over this, vill I?" asked Harold.

"No . . . but ve Lutherans have a proverb:

"There's a little volf in everyone;
Grace comes in being fair
And loving those who sometimes grow
A little extra tooth and hair."

"You know, Martin, the Baptists vill never accept me now!"

Harold found a new way of life among Martin's Lutheran friends, many of whom, like himself, dreaded the full moons. Their lunar fear led many to call them "moonies" because they lived in dread of the full moon.

Martin introduced Harold to his support group. Harold felt a strange camaraderie as he heard Martin stand in the meeting and say to the small, desperate group, "Hello, I'm Martin. I am a volf!"

"Hello, Martin," said the group.

"I have been a volf for thirteen years, seven months, and twenty-three days. But I haven't eaten a Baptist in all these years." The crowd broke into applause.

"Meet Harold," Martin said. "It's his first time at our group." They all greeted Harold with applause. Many of these moonie friends had long struggled with their time of the month. Harold realized he, too, could never brag about being well again, but at least he belonged to a group who understood him.

When he next saw Drusilla, she was on the arm of a new Baptist trapper. "First a volf, then a Lutheran," she sneered at Harold.

"Yes, Drusilla, mein ex-frau, it's true. But I'm a part of a new twelve-step program. I'm dealing with my volfiness one day at a time. I can never be healed, but I am well. Ve've a little proverb, ve volfy Lutherans."

"I never listen to the proverbs of verevolves." Drusilla turned on her heels, sneered, and walked away.

"Vell, Drusilla, I vill give it to you anyway," he shouted after her, and shouted ever louder as she walked away:

"There's a little wolf in everyone
Grace comes in being . . ."

But Drusilla was quickly out of earshot.

The moon turned full that very night, and Harold and Martin roamed the woods searching for life, being very careful to avoid the Baptist traps!

Three years later, Drusilla was out gathering mushrooms when she scratched her hand on a strange thornbush. She cried a bit and stared down at her own hand in horror.

Hair instantly began to grow on her hand. She trembled with fear knowing that her job as a Baptist nursery coordinator was over.

The moon was full that night and Drusilla hurried into the forest, where she met a lot of nice wolves who were dealing with their trauma one full moon at a time.

Drusilla and Harold got back together in the moonie support group. Their love was closer than it ever had been. They were a little hairier than they had been in their younger years, but what's a few extra follicles to those who've been made wise?

And both of them knew well the noblest proverb that Transylvania could boast:

There's a little wolf in everyone
Grace comes in being fair
And loving those who sometimes grow
A little extra tooth and hair.

"How much easier it is to be critical than to be correct."
Benjamin Disraeli, Earl of Beaconsfield, speech given on January 24, 1860

"Do not judge, or you too will be judged. For in the same way you judge others, you will be judged, and with the measure you use, it will be measured to you."
Matthew 7:1-2

"Now that you have purified yourselves by obeying the truth so that you have sincere love for your brothers, love one another deeply from the heart."
1 Peter 1:22

The Night of the Anchovy

The following parable was the result of one of the many interior bouts I have had with televangelism. So much is good about religious television, but its excesses often cause me to indict the good along with the bad. To any who use television for evil purposes, I ask you to read the strange case of Dr. Oneida and his healing. To those whose ministry is altogether wholesome, I offer you only blessings.

Once there was a certain televangelist named Dr. Oneida. Although he constantly told his millions of viewers that they should be filled with joy, he often found himself disconsolate.

"Why are you so depressed?" said Sister Bentley, his assistant, wagging her long finger at him. "You have it all. A worldwide network, a great dandruff shampoo, and a platinum blonde co-host—what else could you possibly want?"

"Well," sighed her boss, "my old jet airplane has only two engines, and it seats only ten people. It's no longer large enough to take our ever-growing crusade team to various cities of the world."

"Well, then, I suggest that you pray for a new vision," Sister Bentley said. "Ask God to give you the desires of your heart. Just name it and claim it. It works for me when I'm out shopping for costume jewelry."

So Dr. Oneida prayed, but no vision came. He prayed even more. Still no vision. He even prayed Saturday after his golf game. Still no vision. So he gave it all up on Saturday night and ordered a Pizza Supreme with jalapeños and anchovies. At last the vision came.

In the vision he saw a beautiful white dove descending on a new twenty-seat plane with four jet engines. In his dream he saw a beautiful woman pilot whose huge white hair was so stiff with hair spray that her coiffure was unruffled by the ear clamps of her headset. Dr. Oneida began to toss and turn in his bed as the jalapeños enraged his euphoria in the middle of the night. Then he heard a loud voice, like the great beast of the Apocalypse. He could not tell if the voice in the vision was rising from below or descending from above. But the message of the voice roared loudly in King James voice—very British and clear: "Go thou and buy this twenty million dollar airplane, that thy glory may flow. Thou shalt soar like lightning in the east, like splendor in the west, like fire in Babylon. Thou shalt name thy plane *Dove I*, and it will be the official airplane of thy worldwide, miracle crusade ministry team."

Dr. Oneida arose inflamed. But his great mood did not last long. He knew his ministry income was not enough to buy *Dove I*. His listeners were not giving enough to buy the plane. He knew what he must do. He must challenge his viewers to love God more. He must say, "Hasn't God healed your diseases? Hasn't God saved your soul? Hasn't God allowed you to name it and claim it? So why do you not love God more and send him your money in care of my zip code?"

At the end of every telecast, he would say, "Dear brothers and sisters, if we do not get more money, our worldwide ministry will be jetless. Jetless! Do you hear me? Jetless and grounded! God has given me a vision of a 900-foot jet plane named *Dove I*. Hallelujah! Shandallah Lear! So, please, please, please give to our 'Wings of Glory' offering so that the turbo-thrust of God's blessing may fall across the runways of the world."

Across the nation, in a small retirement home in Appalachia, there lived a little woman named Sister Felicity who had long been one of the evangelist's supporters. Having grown ill with an incurable illness, she thought to herself, "I must get one of Dr. Oneida's prayer cloths—peradventure God will heal me."

The very night the evangelist told of his vision, Sister Felicity had a vision of her own. In her vision she saw herself in heaven. It was all so wonderful! Still, it introduced a conflict in her life. She had to admit to herself, "While I don't mind being dead, I'm not crazy about dying. Here's what I will do: I will write a letter to Dr. Oneida and this I will say—

"Dear Brother Oneida, here is my life insurance policy. You will notice that I have listed you as the beneficiary. I am not well and probably will not live much longer. All I want in exchange for the policy is one of your wonderful prayer cloths. I'm not quite ready for the Valley of the Shadow yet. Perhaps your cloth will heal me. Here's to the 'Wings of Glory' offering, and may God also give you the turbo-thrust of his blessing."

Dr. Oneida received her letter with great joy. He prayed over a prayer cloth and was about to send it to Sister Felicity when he thought to himself, "Sister Felicity believes so wholeheartedly in Christ. If I pray over this prayer cloth, Christ may actually heal her. Then I will never get the proceeds of her life insurance policy, and lo, I will never get my beautiful new Dove I. What then shall I do? Shall I thwart the will of God by healing her? No, a thousand times no! This will I do: I will send her only a grease rag from Action Garage, which will do her little good, and her untimely death will doubtless speed her insurance money to my global ministry."

When Sister Felicity received the grease rag, she laid it on her frail, old body and asked God to heal her in the name of the Father, the Son, the Holy Spirit, and Dr. Oneida. For her rich faith in the first three, God did indeed heal her. "Glory Hallelujah! Shandallah, non-Lear das kaput," shouted sister Felicity. She could actually feel Dr. Oneida's prayer cloth healing her body. She wrote to the evangelist reporting the miracle.

"Drats!" said Dr. Oneida as he read of her healing. "Drats!" he said, adding a few non-crusade words. Even as he spoke, the scrawling fingers of a man's hand appeared and wrote some strange words around the center cone of his satellite dish: *Meany, Meany, U Takky Parson,* which being interpreted means, "Thou shameful and adulterous televangelist, your kingdom is taken from you. Even your old ten-seater will now be taken away, and the turbo-thrust of my blessings will be given to Sister Ruth on the other network."

In a single night, calamity came. His Nielsen ratings fell, and his cable contract was cancelled.

After years of poverty and honest living, Dr. Oneida received a postal envelope from Sister Felicity one day. It contained the old grease rag that had so miraculously healed her—and a letter:

Dear Dr. Oneida:

I am returning your prayer cloth. It has worked so well that I am feeling great; I am on a Golden-Age tour of the Holy Land with a group of Sister Ruth's supporters.

We climbed the Mount of Olives today—whew!—and bought some olive-wood crosses for everybody in the rest home. If things are quiet on the West Bank tomorrow, we're all going to be baptized in the Jordan.

It sure was too bad that you never got the turbo-thrust of God's blessing. Sister Ruth has it now, you know. She never had a vision of a dove descending on a new plane, but she did have a vision of a flock of Canada geese flying into the engine of a commercial airliner, so she travels mostly by Greyhound.

I hear your ministry has been hurt. You might try laying this prayer cloth on your financial statements. It worked for me!"

Yours for a better tomorrow,
Sister Felicity

P.S. I saw Sister Bentley. Her hair has gone back to its natural color, and she has quit wearing costume jewelry. Has she lost her faith?

Dr. Oneida wept. He knew it was not Sister Bentley who had turned from the faith. He knew that he was the one who had abandoned God's true vision for his life. He looked at the old grease rag. In spite of his own dishonesty, the grease rag had been Sister Felicity's salvation and his ruin.

"God," he said, "I give you this rag in deep repentance. For it has healed a sick woman and condemned an evil man!"

"Not so," said God, "it has healed you both. It has healed a sick woman of her disease and is now healing an egotist of his pride."

"Is there anything I can ever do to repay your kindness?" asked the evangelist.

"Yes. You will know you are completely healed when you have sent ten dollars to Sister Ruth on the other network. She needs money for bus tickets, you know!"

"You have asked a hard thing, God. To confess our pride

is one thing, but to bless our competitors is quite another. Rather, ask me to help in the Adopt-a-Highway program. May I not do this and be clean?"

"You're a slow learner. Must I visit you yet seven times more with boils and scabs?"

Dr. Oneida took ten dollars out of his wallet. He mailed the gift to Sister Ruth, and even as he licked the stamp, he knew at last his sin was purged.

"A good reputation is more valuable than money."
Publilius Syrus, Maxim 108

"The teachers of the law and the Pharisees sit in Moses' seat. So you must obey them and do everything they tell you. But do not do what they do, for they do not practice what they preach. . . . They love the place of honor at banquets and the most important seats in the synagogues. . . . The greatest among you will be your servant. For whoever exalts himself will be humbled, and whoever humbles himself will be exalted."
Matthew 23:2-3, 6, 11-12

"People who want to get rich fall into temptation and a trap and into many foolish and harmful desires that plunge men into ruin and destruction. For the love of money is a root of all kinds of evil. Some people, eager for money, have wandered from the faith and pierced themselves with many griefs. . . . Command those who are rich in this present world not to be arrogant nor to put their hope in wealth, which is so uncertain, but to put their hope in God, who richly provides us with everything for our enjoyment."
1 Timothy 6:9-10, 17

Apple Cora

Sin is serious business, but then so is grace. Which is the most serious, I cannot say for sure, but grace is my preference.

A certain priest stopped every morning on his way to hear confessions and stole an apple from an orchard that he passed. On the orchard wall was a sign that clearly said, "Keep Out, No Pilfering!" Nonetheless the priest would always steal a piece of fruit and eat it on the way to hear confessions. He always finished the apple just before he entered the confessional, throwing the core on his side of the curtain.

A certain young girl named Cora also stopped every morning on her way to confession and stole an apple. Just as she stepped into the confessional, she would finish it and throw the core on her side of the curtain.

"Bless me, Father, for I have sinned," she would say.

"How long has it been, my child, since your last confession?"

"Twenty-four hours!"

"And is your sin the same today as usual?"

"It is, Father. I am still stealing apples on the way to confession!"

"*Te absolvo* . . . but I warn you, give up those apples, you silly girl, or you will someday boil in cider for a thousand years!"

Cora would quake at his chilling judgment. "I'll try, Father, I'll try. But the apples are so good and I am so weak."

Every day the ritual was repeated. Every twenty-four hours, the priest stole another, and so did Cora.

Finally the priest grew exasperated with Cora.

"Bless me, Father, for I have sinned," she said one very ordinary morning.

"Today, Cora, I refuse to forgive you. You keep on stealing, and I'm tired of forgiving you for what we both know you will do again. You'll never change, you wretched girl. Henceforth, I do not forgive you."

"Please Father. I'm so very sorry."

"No, before the cider dries upon your chinny-chin-chin, you steal and pick and eat again. I counted 365 decaying cores on your side of the confessional. You are too wicked and apple-ridden to receive my forgiveness any longer!"

The girl wept her way from the confessional. She cried until 10:35 that morning.

Her guilt grew for weeks and she finally quit coming to confessional.

Hypocrisy seemed to curse the land. The fields around the church turned brown. The swans left the pond. The early daylight was dull and gray. The land seemed to die even as the priest kept stealing the forbidden fruit. Finally, the apples in the orchard were very few, and mostly in the top of the trees. The wretched girl, still unable to leave her addiction, shinnied up to the highest frost-tinged boughs. She was about to pick an apple when she noticed some movement in the branches across from her. Then she noticed a black cassock.

"Father, what are you doing here?" asked Cora.

"Praying," said the priest.

"In an apple tree?" asked the girl.

"Yes, my dear, to be closer to heaven!"

"Oh, that I came here to pray. I came only to steal apples!"

"Wretch!" screamed the priest.

At that very instant, the limb on which he was supported broke and the priest plummeted to the ground. Cora scrambled down and ran to see if the priest was dead.

"Girl, I am dying. You must give me last rites!"

"No, Father. I am impure, filled with harried and vile and unforgiven apple thieveries. I am too wicked to grant you the absolution that you need. May God have mercy on you, Father."

The priest died and burned in flaming cider, but of course Cora never knew.

A new priest came a few weeks later, and Cora started back to church. Once again she went to confessional.

"Bless me, Father, for I have sinned. I stole an apple this morning on the way to church."

"You, too?" said the priest. "Tomorrow morning let's both steal three and we shall make a pie together. Who knows but what our Father in heaven shall provide the cinnamon."

Then at last the swans came back and the fields turned green.

And when Cora and the priest had eaten many a pie, they found they actually began to help each other deal with their sins. They leaned on each other and prayed for each other, and finally both were able to quit stealing apples. (They did not steal them all that often, at least.) Still, some sins are hard to quit, and in order to avoid temptation, the kindest apple thieves always help each other pass the best orchards.

"The hypocrite's crime is that he bears false witness against himself."
Hannah Arendt, *On Revolution*

"You hypocrites! Isaiah was right when he prophesied about you: 'These people honor me with their lips, but their hearts are far from me.'"
Matthew 15:7-8

"But the wisdom that comes from heaven is first of all pure; then peace-loving, considerate, submissive, full of mercy and good fruit, impartial and sincere."
James 3:17

The Wicked Man

A certain wicked man took advantage of people and used them to get his own ends. He was brutal and unfair in all his dealings. One day while bicycling across the Bay Bridge, he fell in. Not knowing how to swim, he cried out to God, "God, help! Save me!"

A huge hand came out of the sky and put him back on the bridge.

He was so happy to be alive that he began to sing "God of Our Fathers." But within a little while he was back, working crooked business deals and cheating people in order to get rich.

One day as he motored along in his Porsche, he ran into a lorry that smashed up his car and sent him to the hospital.

"You have a giant hematoma," said the doctor. "You cannot live. I'm sorry, we've done all we can."

The doctor left the room and the man prayed earnestly. "God, help! Save me!"

"You again!" said God.

"I know I've not been too steadfast, but God, it's this hematoma! Will you take it away?"

"I don't know. You know, the last time I saved you, it just didn't work out."

"Please God, I'll do anything!"

"Will you be a Baptist?"

"Okay, okay."

"Hematoma, begone!" said the voice from the sky.

The doctors were amazed when they next entered his room. He was eating jello and singing "God of Our Fathers."

The hematoma was gone and the man was dismissed.

He did become a Baptist, but not a very good one. And in a little while, he was back dabbling in unsupported securities and gigging clients with dishonest claims. He was committed to making the bucks, whatever he had to do to get them.

One day while on a routine flight, he made a right turn in the service bay of a 747, mistakenly thinking it was the bathroom door, and plunged headlong into space.

"Help God!" he cried. "Help, help!"

"You again!" said the voice from the sky.

A huge hand came out of the clouds and grabbed him by the collar. "Look, buster!" said God. "First the Bay Bridge, then the hematoma, now this! I'm not altogether convinced that you have been worth the saving."

"Look, God, if you let me down easy, I'll not only be a Baptist, but a Baptist deacon. I'll sing in the choir and take my turn in the nursery."

"Promise?" asked God.

"Scout's honor," said the frightened man.

The giant hand from the clouds set him down in the parking lot of a Baptist church on Sunday night.

"Now, get with it!" said the giant voice.

He went into the Baptist church. In a few months he had become a deacon. He even took his turn in the nursery. And he suddenly realized how much money could be made right there among these brothers and sisters. So he lapsed back into his dishonest ways and soon was cheating and stealing and working his shady deals right in the church.

Well, it happened on a Thursday that a mugger on a dark street shoved a knife hard against his back and said, "Your money or your life!"

"Help, God, help!"

There was no voice from the sky.

"God, if you save me, I'll give you ten percent of all I've got in my pocket."

There was still no voice from the sky.

"Okay, God, twenty-five and three-quarters. Is that fair or what?"

There was no voice from heaven.

"Your money or your life," said the mugger, "and I mean *now*!"

"Shove off, punk! Who do you think you are, God?"

The mugger said nothing, but he did shove the knife a little more tautly against the rib cage and began singing "God of Our Fathers."

"Hypocrisy is the homage that vice pays to virtue."
François, Duc de La Rochefoucauld,
Reflections or *Sentences and Moral Maxims*

"Jesus answered, 'I am the way and the truth and the life.'"
John 14:6

"Again, you have heard that it was said to the people long ago, 'Do not break your oath, but keep the oaths you have made to the Lord."
Matthew 5:33

"Delight yourself in the LORD and he will give you the desires of your heart. Commit your way to the LORD; trust in him and he will do this: He will make your righteousness shine like the dawn, the justice of your cause like the noonday sun."
Psalm 37:4-6

The Shawl of Paul and the Book of God

On Relics and the Real Thing

The Shawl of Paul

Relics have a way of eclipsing the adoration that ought to be given to God. The fervor that developed over the shroud of Turin awoke this story that long slept in my cynical soul.

Once upon a time a poor woman ordered a simple cassock for her husband. When the robe came, it bore a label that read "Penney's Terry-Cloth Office of Sales"—or P.T.C.O.S., for short.

Her husband wore it for a few years and then put it in a missions barrel for his church. An aging cleric took the robe from the barrel and stuck it behind a loose brick in the vestry wall. He intended to save it for himself—but having a sudden stroke, he passed on to his reward.

A few years later, Father Ignatius, a humble monk, happened to notice a loose stone in the back wall of Chapel 13. When he slipped the brick from its place, he saw behind it a crude cloth which he pulled out. It was very primitive cloth, which he believed to be third-century in origin. It bore an early Greek laundry mark, "P.T.C.O.S.," which he took to mean "Paul of Tarsus, Chief of Sinners."

He fell on his face and cried four words: "The Shawl of Paul!"

He brought in a team of experts who did an inconclusive pollen count from the fibers and concluded that the shawl might be first-century, and might actually have belonged to the Apostle Paul.

Father Ignatius was delirious with delight. He went on tour with the Shawl of Paul and charged interested onlookers five dollars to see it. Overnight, Father Ignatius became very famous for the shawl.

One night the president of CBS had the monk on a network show and asked him if there was any doubt that this was the true Shawl of Paul. "No doubt," said Father Ignatius.

Then the president of ABC had him on a network show and asked him if it wasn't true that the Shawl of Paul was really much earlier in origin, and that this robe couldn't possibly have belonged to the biblical character.

The answer was always the same. "This is indeed the Shawl of Paul."

One night the Apostle Paul appeared to Ignatius in a vision and spoke only four words: "It's not mine, Ignatius!"

Father Ignatius was now confused. Should he tell the truth and end his wonderful whirlwind of international acclaim? He knew that being honest might destroy his income. He finally decided to call the presidents of CBS and ABC.

"Either of you hear from the Apostle Paul?"

"No," said the president of CBS.

"No," said the president of ABC. "Why?"

"Oh, nothing," said Ignatius. "Nothing at all." So the secret was safe. The deception could go on blessing the world and keeping Ignatius in the chips. He had just decided to up his rates when his phone rang.

"Father Ignatius? The president of NBC here. The Apostle Paul just appeared to me in a vision, and I'd like to have you on one of our shows," smirked the executive into the receiver. Father Ignatius hung up!

"What dire offense from amorous causes springs;
what mighty contests rise from trivial things!"
Alexander Pope, *The Rape of the Lock*

"There is no calamity greater than lavish desires.
There is no greater guilt than discontentment.
And there is no greater disaster than greed."
Lao-tzu, *The Way of Lao-tzu*

"God is spirit, and his worshipers must worship in spirit and in truth."
John 4:24

"Woe to them! They have taken the way of Cain; they have rushed for
profit into Balaam's error; they have been destroyed in Korah's rebellion."
Jude 11

"How useless to spread a net in full view of all the birds!"
Proverbs 1:17

"Such is the end of all who go after ill-gotten gain; it takes away the lives
of those who get it."
Proverbs 1:19

"Rather, we have renounced secret and shameful ways; we do not use
deception, nor do we distort the word of God. On the contrary, by setting
forth the truth plainly we commend ourselves to every man's conscience in
the sight of God."
2 Corinthians 4:2

"If anyone teaches false doctrines and does not agree to the sound
instruction of our Lord Jesus Christ and to godly teaching he is
conceited and understands nothing."
1 Timothy 6:3-4

The Book of God

In protest of those scholars who know their instruments of surgery but have rarely spoken to their patients.

The Book! The Book!
That was, and is,
And will be evermore.
Born in realms removed.
Old as uncooled moons
But young in every age of man.
Emanating from the center of the middle—
The pulp and fiber of all being.
There in starry volumes
For eternity,
But falling on us gently,
One letter at a time.
Near print on near paper,
Whispered messages in ink
From our longing, upward, distant lover.

Distant? Never.
Words born here in time
Yet hatched
In languageless infinity.
God wearing syllables,
That leap from new formed-clay
To papyrus and codex—
From whispered wind to printed word.
Sing! God has a stylus in His hands!

He shouts in quill and ink,
"Here I am
Within this Book,
This Book of Books,
This word incomparable,
This vellum band surpassing excellence,
This scroll majestic.
Here is my majesty
In common nouns and verbs
I gave to babes and warlords,
To Aramaic shepherds
And Hittite vagabonds,
To Hebrew, Greek, and Latin monks,
To Elizabethan scholars,
And best of all, to you.

In this book I come
Whispering in ink,
Breathing,
Revealing,
Disclosing,
Never quitting!
All bright determined,
My aching silence shouts:
I have a Son.
My once begotten
Is the center of this Shaddai papyrus.
It is living ink.
Hold it to your ear
Like the conch of YHWH
And you will hear the Red Sea roar—

The rattle of iron rims on cobblestones—
The neighing of war horses—
The soft tread of camels in the sand—
The snap of breaking loaves—
The clear, clean song of lepers
Welcome in the streets.

Listen to the warm!
Almighty love is
Resonating through the Pentateuch,
Swelling in the histories,
Bursting symphonically
In Psalms of timpani
And flutes above the misty seas.
Can you hear
These thrumming cadences?
These brassy fanfares of the Easter news?

Our God can write!
He lifts his starry quill,
And the ages beg for parchment.
A thousand pages
Of Adam's sad biography,
And on each one,
The grace-drawn portrait
Of his son.
His words, wide as Andromeda,
Stir the artist to create,
The compassionate to care,
The disconsolate to laughter,
The mute to oratorios,

The paralytics into fervent dancing.
The word, the word!
The singing, distant word!
Jehovah in a pen nib,
Writing in such fire
As warms the grave,
Writing with the ink of human tears
To quench the fires of Hell,
The present poetry of suffering.
The promised prose of hope,
Settling on us
Like a sparrow,
Small and inobtrusive
Like a dove
Pure in its intent,
Like an eagle
Visible and powerful.

This Book is ours—
Illustrated
With a thousand etchings
Of the face of God—
Burning through our weak morality,
Then, like a new, born sun
Ordered into sky—
Circling the earth
And orbiting our private world in light.

"The English Bible—a book which if everything else in our language should perish, would alone suffice to show the whole extent of its beauty and power."
Thomas Babington, Lord Macaulay, *On John Dryden*

"I tell you the truth, until heaven and earth disappear, not the smallest letter, not the least stroke of a pen, will by any means disappear from the Law until everything is accomplished. . . . Heaven and earth will pass away, but my words will never pass away."
Matthew 5:18; 24:35

"For the word of God is living and active. Sharper than any double-edged sword, it penetrates even to dividing soul and spirit, joints and marrow; it judges the thoughts and attitudes of the heart."
Hebrews 4:12

"The grass withers and the flowers fall, but the word of our God stands forever."
Isaiah 40:8

Friday and Sunday

Pull out the nails from his gripless hands;
Loosen the ropes from the shoulders of a man;
Take Him from the wood and lay Him on the sand.
He is dead—it is Friday—He is dead!

The woman who is weeping said He was her Son;
Said He was forepromised as the Mighty One;
Thirty years of motherhood, all undone.
Weep, little mother—He is dead.

Prostitutes and publicans, weep and rave;
Your King who gave you life is ready for the grave;
Lay your Messiah in a cold, dark cave.
Weep, you hapless orphans—He is dead.

"Dead," moaned the chilling April wind;
"Dead," sobbed the Pharisee who was His friend;
Dead—immortality has met its end.
Eternal life is done with—He is dead.

All of you fishers, return to the sea;
You were His disciples until Calvary;
Weep your weary way back to Galilee.
He has cried, "It is finished," and is dead.

The promises of victory have ended in defeat;
Friday's Conqueror has pierced feet;
He is bound in a shroud and a winding sheet.
The Carpenter of Nazareth is dead.

(Then came Sunday)

Look! Shafts of sunlight have driven back the night!
Look at the Master clothed in iridescent white!
Look at the women falling back in fright!
He's alive—It is Sunday—He's alive!

Rejoice, James and John and Simon of Cyrene,
Peter, Nicodemus, and Mary Magdalene!
Annas and Cleopas the risen Lord have seen.
He is living—He is living—He's alive!

Oh, Thomas, Thomas, why do you doubt?
Thrust in your hand where the spear came out;
This is not a fantasy. Lift the joyous shout.
He is living—He is living—He's alive!

Flourish the trumpets; the living Saviour comes!
Roll the victory cadence on a thousand drums!
Let the anthem swell from a thousand tongues!
He is living—He is living—He's alive!

"Beneath this sod
A poet lies, or that which once seemed he—
Oh, lift a thought in prayer for S.T.C.!
That he, who many a year, with toil of breath,
Found death in life, may here find life in death."
Samuel Taylor Coleridge, epitaph written for himself

"Jesus said to her, 'I am the resurrection and the life. He who believes in me will live, even though he dies.'"
John 11:25

"Praise be to the God and Father of our Lord Jesus Christ! In his great mercy he has given us new birth into a living hope through the resurrection of Jesus Christ from the dead."
1 Peter 1:3

Bible Man

Lois Schwarz had been married to Clark Schwarz for two years before she began to suspect that Clark was really Bible Man. One Thursday night, she found a pair of blue leotards in the clothes hamper.

"Yours?" she asked Clark.

"Uh-huh," he confessed, looking down.

"Clark . . ." she paused, "can you leap tall steeples in a single bound? Are you faster than a speeding Lear jet full of cable evangelists?"

It was all true.

"Honey," Clark said, "since you know now, would you promise not to tell a soul? And maybe you could wash my costume here at home. Remember, don't put the red tights with the blue leotards," he blushed.

That's how Lois found out. At first she felt proud that her husband was Bible Man. She was thrilled just knowing that he could run into the smallest church, throw off his Dockers and tweedy coat, and be Bible Man. Only his Oakwood High class ring (which no one ever seemed to notice) told the world that he was simply Clark Schwarz.

Still, Bible Man never missed a chance to help out in his needy world.

When a couple was about to get a divorce, he would crash through their front window and hand them a card that said, "Divorce not, but grow in grace." On the back of such cards always appeared a list of relevant Scriptures.

If a man was about to cheat on his income tax, Bible Man would crash through the ceiling at just the right moment with a card that said, "Cheat not, for the soul that cheateth shall die." On the back of the card, to be sure, was a well-researched index of Scriptures, forbidding dishonesty.

At first, Lois felt good laundering his costumes and keeping his cards ready. But before long, she felt uneasy with Clark. For one thing, Clark had begun to wear his costume around the house, and was becoming a little wearisome. One afternoon when she was vegging out before an afternoon TV talk show, he gave her a card that said, "Watch not, lest thine eyes corrupt thee."

He also gave her a card one Tuesday night after finding out that she had given a plastic-container party for her friends. The card read, "Tupper not, thou whited sepulcher." Bit by bit, Lois tired of her superhero.

But Lois wasn't the only one affected. As Clark became more and more self-righteous, he found he could scarcely leap Pentecostal churches. He inevitably snagged his leotards on high Episcopal spires. Finally his leotards were so full of runs, his ministry began to lose ground in public opinion polls.

One night while he was off on a flight to rebuke a Baptist with a "Drink not" card, and an Episcopalian with a "Gamble not" card, Lois packed up and left. She called the *New York Times* and blew Clark's cover. He was furious with Lois. "How could you?" he screamed at her.

She handed him a small card. "Fume not," it read, "rather love your wife so that when your days on earth are over, you may be received into eternal habitations." There were a lot of Scriptures on the back of the card.

"For we must consider that we shall be as a city upon a hill. The eyes of all people are upon us, so that if we shall deal falsely without God in this work we have undertaken and so cause Him to withdraw His present help from us, we shall be made a story and a byword through the world."
John Winthrop, *A Model of Christian Charity*

"Man is no angel. He is sometimes
more of a hypocrite and sometimes less."
Honoré de Balzac

"You diligently study the Scriptures because you think that by them you possess eternal life. These are the Scriptures that testify about me."
John 5:39

"Is not my word like fire," declares the LORD, "and like a hammer that breaks a rock in pieces?"
Jeremiah 23:29

"Though he slay me, yet will I trust him: but I will maintain my own ways before him. He also shall be my salvation: for an hypocrite shall not come before him."
Job 13:15-16 (KJV)

"The joy of the hypocrite is but for a moment."
Job 20:5 (KJV)

"The teachers of the law and the Pharisees sit in Moses seat. So you must do everything they tell you. But do not do what they do, for they do not practice what they preach."
Matthew 23:2-3

The Old 100th Revisited

Gratitude really is an attitude, and thanksgiving isn't just for November. This piece and the one which appears on page 121 were written many years apart.

"Make a joyful noise unto the Lord."
To waken those who've lost the voice of praise.
Set your joyful noise free
And loosen all
Your up-tight propriety,
Your thumb-worn impiety,
Your dull sobriety.
Release your need to think well of who you are
Till you find the abandon to love Him for who He is,
Rejoice!

"All ye lands."
No lands may be exempt.
All must praise.
Lands torn by war
Must patch their shredded banners and rejoice.
Fat lands who overeat and underpray.
Thin lands where broth is weak and rice is rationed.

"Worship the Lord with gladness."
A gladness unrestrained by sensibility.
A loud-mouthed gladness which will not be shushed.
A manly gladness whose laughter never degenerates to silliness.
A gladness God gives to still the weeping heart.

"Come before His presence with singing."
No apathetic anthems.
No devotion held in the tiny buckets of the cautious.
No paltry praise.
No skinny hymns.

"Know ye that the Lord, He is God."
A welcome God is He for all the godless.
A powerful Lord is He for all the weak.
A Lord triumphant for the beaten and despised.

"It is He who has made us."
We are fearfully and wonderfully made.
We have a Maker.
We did not happen on the planet.
We were not born in cosmic accidents.
We are more than sunlight or pond scum.
We are made—He did it!

"And not we ourselves."
No creature is his own God.
No man formed his own soul.
No woman called her own life into being.

"We are His people."
Look at us!
Multi-colored,
Multi-national,
Multi-talented,
Multi-spirited,
Yet universal and unique.

"The sheep of His pasture."
Black sheep seeking better wool,
Hungry sheep looking for green pastures,
Thirsty sheep looking for still waters,
Terrified sheep bleating our insecurities.
Still, His rod and staff—they comfort us!

"Enter into His gates with thanksgiving."
Be thankful in all things.
Be thankful *for* all things.
Now thank we all our God
With heart and soul and voices,
Whom wondrous things have done,
In whom our world rejoices.

"And into His courts with praise."
His courts hold the symphonies of our souls.
Sing alleluia to the throne—
Praise God! He is Father!
Praise Jesus! He is Savior!
Praise the Spirit! He indwells us!

"Give thanks to Him."
Thanks, Thanks, Thanks!
Thanks for the good stuff,
Thanks for the sweet stuff,
Thanks for the hard stuff,
Thanks for the tears that clear our vision.
Thanks for the darkness that makes us cherish light.

"And praise His name!"
Say: Holy, Holy, Holy,
Lord God Almighty.
Early in the morning, our song shall rise to Thee.

"For the Lord is good."
Good beyond all reckoning,
Good beyond all measuring,
Good beyond all questioning,
Good!

"His love endures forever."
When clocks have hidden all their numbered dials
And lifeless pendulums hang dead;
When the sun no longer spins to measure days,
God's love will still hold place,
More faithful than the fickle pole star,
More certain than inconstant constellations,
Forever there, forever love.

"And His faithfulness continues to all generations."
Great is thy faithfulness, O God my Father.
There is no shadow of turning with Thee.
Thou changest not, Thy compassions they fail not.
As Thou has been, Thou forever wilt be.
Summer and winter and springtime and harvest,
Sun, moon, and stars in their courses above,
Join with all nature in manifold witness
To thy great faithfulness, mercy, and love.

"Selah!"

"Sweet is the breath of vernal shower,
The bee's collected treasures sweet,
Sweet music's melting fall, but sweeter yet
The still small voice of gratitude."
Thomas Gray, *Ode for Music*

"Ingratitude, thou marble-hearted friend."
William Shakespeare, *King Lear*

"Jesus asked, 'Where not all ten cleansed? Where are the other nine?
Was no one found to return and give praise to God except this foreigner?'
Then he said to him, 'Rise and go; your faith has made you well.'"
Luke 17:17-19

"O LORD, open my lips, and my mouth will declare your praise."
Psalm 51:15

"On your feet now—applaud God!
Bring a gift of laughter,
sing yourselves into his presence.
Know this: God is God, and God, God.
He made us; we didn't make him.
We're his people, his well-tended sheep.
Enter with the password: 'Thank you!'
Make yourselves at home, talking praise.
Thank him. Worship him.
For God is sheer beauty,
all-generous in love,
loyal always and ever."
Psalm 100 (The Message)

"In every thing give thanks: for this is the will of God in Christ Jesus
concerning you."
1 Thessalonians 5:18 (KJV)

Section 4

Once Upon a Time, Jesus

Parables for Postmoderns

79

Penteuchio

Some years ago in reading one of my favorite theologians, I was struck with the concept of "The Burden of God," as he had entitled the monograph. When God created human beings and set them on the earth with the gift of free will, he endowed his creatures with the ultimate power to reject even himself, the very God who had fashioned them in the first place. This allegory resulted from my own reckoning with the "Burden of God."

In a small hamlet of Germany, as the sixteenth century was drawing to a close, there lived an aging and childless rabbi named Japheth ben Levi. One Thursday, as he was reading the Pentateuch, he began to weep. He pulled his prayer shawl far forward over his face and waited for the tears to stop. But alas, his tears would not stop.

"God, I am sorry to come to you crying, like so much of the world customarily does, but my grievance is too long for a letter and too heavy to wait any longer. God, I must ask you this: Is it right that you should have made yourself a whole world of children and that Esther and I should be condemned to live alone? Your children are as the sands of the sea, yet we have no inheritance at all.

"Further, your children are not well behaved. And while I hate to point this out to you, many of your kids are giving you a bad name, what being murderers and malcontents and loud-mouthed politicians. If you would give us a son, I promise you that my son would turn out no worse than some of yours have."

"Why talk to me like this, Japheth?" said God, at last, "If you think my family has too many brigands and cutthroats, consider that I have also created an ungrateful and loud-mouthed rabbi or two."

Japheth said nothing. Things tend to get quiet when God isn't.

After a while, God spoke once again, "You have a father but no son, Japheth, am I right?"

"You are right, God! You are always right!"

"Then you know the work of being a child, am I right?"

"You are right, of course, God. You are always right!"

"But you do not know the really hard work of being a father. Am I right?"

"Yes, God, always and ever you are right, which I might add makes your work easier than mine!"

"Do not sass me, my child. I am going to give you off-spring."

"But how can this be? I am old and Esther is as barren as a desert."

"Do you have a table leg?"

"Yes, I do, God. You know I do. I have four table legs which are on our table, keeping it far enough from the floor to hold our simple meals."

"Well, take one leg off your table and whittle out a mari-onette."

"But, God, if I take a leg off the table, it will teeter and be unstable."

"Why talk to me, Japheth? Do you think any real miracles can occur when the whole world is stable? Why should you be allowed to sit at a stable table while all heaven is in an uproar? Do you want a son or not?"

"To be sure."

"Then, Japheth, you must whittle."

"Yes, God."

As soon as God got through talking to the rabbi, lightning flashed. And that was about all that happened on Thursday.

Upon entering the kitchen on Friday morning and seeing Japheth sawing a leg off her table, his wife, Esther, demanded, "What are you doing to my table?"

"Why talk to me, Esther? I am only obeying the Almighty," said the rabbi as he continued sawing.

"So God doesn't like this table either. I told you it was ugly when we bought it."

"Esther, I have some wonderful news. God wants me to carve out a marionette, which in time will become our son."

"In a pig's eye!"

"I forbid you to use such unkosher epithets!" said Japheth.

"Forgive me, but why would God give us a son when his own children behave so badly?"

"I mentioned that to him. He said parenting is harder work than we imagine."

The table leg was suddenly sawed through. It fell to the floor and hit the rabbi's foot.

"Oww, God!" yelled the rabbi as he turned his eyes to the ceiling and began holding his injured foot while hopping around the room on the other. "That hurt, God," he yelled to the ceiling.

"Why talk to me, Japheth? Do you think you can bring children into the world without pain?" asked God.

Japheth said nothing else. He sat down almost immediately and began to carve. "What shall I call you, little one?" he said to the still unshaped table leg. "I know. Since I first complained of my childlessness while reading the Pentateuch, I shall call you Penteuchio."

In so simple a way was the table leg given a name, and the name stuck.

As he carved, Japheth would talk to the table leg, and day by day it looked less and less like a table leg and more and more like a marionette.

On the fourth week the rabbi had carved down past the marionettes eyes, and as he did so, the eyes snapped suddenly alive. They darted around the room as though they were looking for what mischief they might cause. This so unnerved the old rabbi that he tied an old sock around Penteuchio's eyes so his skitterish glances would be hidden from the craftsman. With the eyes covered Japheth continued his work, and by the sixth week he had carved down past the head, setting the chin free at last to move.

"Hi ya, Daddio!" said Penteuchio.

"I am your father. You must not speak to me in such a manner! Do you hear me, young man?"

"I'll call you what I please," said the insolent marionette.

Japheth found another old sock and stuck it in the insolent mouth of his sassy creation.

"Mffft!" said Penteuchio, trying to talk with a sock wedged between his wooden lips. Japheth faced a quandary. Should he go on with this desperate dream or throw his partially formed son into the fireplace? The battle raged as he turned to God.

"God, should I go on with this or not? It seems Penteuchio may turn out badly."

"Why talk to me, Japheth? This is the burden of all makers,

my child. Who can say how a sock-in-the-mouth boy will turn out? When I first made my boy Adam, I should have put a sock in his mouth. You know what the Book says: I gave him a thousand orchards, and he picked the only tree I told him he couldn't have. You need to think this over, Japheth. Keep the sock in his mouth. Go and put the table leg in the corner, fix yourself a bagel, and have a talk with Esther about family planning before you go any further."

So Japheth put Penteuchio in a bag and set him in the corner. "Should we go on with this or not, Esther? I have reason to believe our little Penteuchio will know more of sin than salvation. He is not even made, and already he is sassy and sour!"

"Why talk to me, Japheth? It was you who wanted an heir and a son, and now on the brink of having one, would you throw the whole thing in the fire?"

So on into the future weeks, the rabbi carved and quoted Scripture. At week ten, when the arms came free, one of Penteuchio's arms lashed out and grabbed a carving knife and jammed it in Japheth's leg. Japheth impulsively cried out, "Oww!" Then he grabbed up an old sock and lashed it around the doll's arms and tied it tightly behind his back.

"Japheth," said God, laughing, "how can one little boy have so many socks and no feet as yet? Your boy isn't turning out so well, is he?"

"Why talk to me, God? You think Ghenghis Khan and Nero were any better?"

As long as Japheth kept Penteuchio's arms tied securely down, the carving went well. And by the fifteenth week, all the carving was at last done and the marionette was complete. But as the legs were set free, then pinned into place, Penteuchio lashed out with his little oak legs, kicking his maker again and again. It was only with great difficulty that the rabbi managed to lash them together with yet another sock. After the final sock had been drawn tightly around the marionette's legs, Japheth put him in a wooden box and set a huge, heavy stone on him.

Then he looked down at him and began to weep. "Ah, my little Penteuchio! How I should like to take all your binding away and set you free. But I am afraid you would do me much mischief. What evil you must hold within your tiny oaken heart." He blew out the lamp and left his orphaned son there in the dark.

"Esther," said the old man, entering their bedroom, "our boy is done. He's under a huge stone and bound and gagged. I haven't the slightest hope that upon liberating him he will do us honor."

"Well, you can't keep him gagged and under stone for the rest of his life, Japheth."

"I know. In the morning, Esther, I'll consider what to do about him."

Esther slept poorly; Japheth, not at all. He woke early the next morning and sat down at the table once more, where he heard a familiar voice:

"Japheth, this is God . . ."

"I know . . ."

"You've got to let him go, you know."

"But, what if he disowns me and embarrasses me or makes me cry for the sheer size of his disobedience? What will I do then?"

"Why talk to me, Japheth? I had a daughter—my first daughter—who ran off with a snake and then gave birth to a murderer. I tell you, it's much easier to *make* children than to set them free. But you can't create them to be free and then tie them up with socks and keep them under rocks. I didn't do that to Adam, and I didn't do that to you. So, Japheth, now you know the burden of God, do you not?"

God became quiet, and old Japheth sat for two hours, wrangling over what it meant to love an unlovely little creature. There was no question about it: he did love Penteuchio. With everything in him, he desired to set him free. So with all his strength, he stood up and walked across the room and lifted the lid on the box. He took the stone off his wooden son. Then he took away the old sock that covered the boy's eyes. Those strange little eyes squinted their wooden lids to adjust to the light. As his eyes were now free to look about, his tiny wooden ears were free to hear, and so the old man spoke.

"Tell me this, my little one: if I take the gag out of your mouth, will you speak honorably?"

The marionette nodded in assent.

The gag was removed.

"Oh, father . . ." said the boy. The very word brought tears of joy to the soul of old Japheth. "I love you. Please take the socks from my arms and I will embrace you."

Japheth, having waited all his life for such an embrace, quickly complied. The sock came off and the boy's thin oak arms shot upward and fell around the thick neck of his maker and father.

"Oh, father, if you but take the cords from my legs, I will walk with you to synagogue."

Again, Japheth's clumsy but warm hands took the sock that bound the legs of his little one. The boy leapt from his lap and danced about the room singing, "I'm free! I'm free! I am forever free!" His delight was so great that the old man took his little wooden fingers in his own and the two of them danced around the room.

But the old man's merriment was short-lived, for in but a moment, the boy shook free of his grasp and ran toward the low burning embers of the fireplace. He reached into the fire, grabbed a burning log, and tossed it into the kindling box. In a moment there was fire everywhere, and while the old man worked at getting the fire under control, Penteuchio leapt out the window and hurried off into the night. The house was saved, but Japheth's little wooden boy was lost. Japheth wept and resigned himself to childlessness.

~~

As time went on, Penteuchio widely denied that Japheth had ever been his father or maker. And Japheth, sad and dis-couraged, having lived longer than old brokenhearted men should have to live, said during his final year of life, "God, you told me to set him free—and I did—but now this very son I made denies that I ever made him."

"So, Japheth, many of Adam's children treat me with the same denials. You have learned the burden of God. You freed your child. If it hurts, then you must know how often through the ages I have known the cost of refusing to put a rock on Adam. Japheth, children are the glorious burdens of my never-dying hope of making earth a little more like heaven."

Three hundred years have passed since Japheth was laid to rest in that little German cemetery. But even today, those who live in that little German town believe that heaven's highest throne has right beside it a small wicker chair. There, the great God and a wizened rabbi often sit and talk about the high cost of creating children and setting them free. But the joy of that wonderful place has been made wise by earthly pain. And heaven's truths have all been proved on a blue-white planet where some children still steal old men's dreams . . . and others eat fruit that is forbidden.

"It is a wise father that knows his own child."
William Shakespeare, *The Merchant of Venice*

"Yet to all who received him, to those who believed in his name, he gave the right to become children of God."
John 1:12

"Those who are led by the Spirit of God are sons of God. For you did not receive a spirit that makes you a slave again to fear, but you received the Spirit of sonship. And by him we cry, 'Abba, Father.'"
Romans 8:14-15

"We know that the whole creation has been groaning as in the pains of childbirth right up to the present time. Not only so, but we ourselves, who have the firstfruits of the Spirit, groan inwardly as we wait eagerly for our adoption as sons, the redemption of our bodies."
Romans 8:22-23

Sleeping Ugly

In a world where Barbie and Ken define what's acceptable in physical attractiveness, God calls out for true beauty—the loveliness of servanthood that is more than skin deep.

Once upon a time, in a faraway land, there lived a king named Olaf and his expectant queen named Bunsie. The last name of the royal family was Sturdley, but the king and queen never used it. The king didn't like last names, and the queen just didn't like the sound of Bunsie Sturdley.

There was, as usual, a good fairy. She was named Bonnie. For a good fairy, Bonnie was typically good at changing some things into other things, but she was not very good at telling the future.

One morning, after she had put on her make-up (good fairies always wear a lot of blush and warm beige base), she went into the throne room to make a prediction to the king and queen.

"Your Majesties!" she began in a loud voice, "I predict that you will have a very lovely child."

It seemed a safe enough prediction, for she did not say whether it would be a boy or girl. She also used the word "lovely." This seemed safe, too, for what parents do not think their baby lovely.

The next morning at seven o'clock, the queen had her baby. "Yee-gad!" said the doctor when he saw it.

"Is it a boy or a girl?" asked the queen.

"Yes," replied the doctor, as he handed the newborn baby to King Olaf.

"Yee-Gad!" said the King. Queen Bunsie could tell by the way everyone said "Yee-Gad!" instead of "How lovely!" that her child must have been less beautiful than she had hoped for.

"Olaf, dearie, is it a boy or a girl?" asked Queen Bunsie.

"It's too early to tell!" said the king.

Well, that's how Dru-Ella Sturdley (for they named her after her old Uncle Andrew and her old aunt Ella) entered the world. The baby was so ugly that King Olaf made Bonnie, the good fairy, stand in the corner for two weeks for her "false prophecy!"

They had the royal artist paint several pictures of the new baby but wisely kept them under lock and key. Even Queen Bunsie was not overly proud of her little Dru-Ella.

The royal doctor said that she might grow out of it in time, but it turned out not to be so. Bunsie taught Dru-Ella to crochet, which was most helpful during her dating years—when she didn't.

It was during these years that Dru-Ella began to love the homeless. She would often stand for hours passing out cookies to hungry children on the street. She especially liked reading to the blind, who never said "Yee-Gad!" when she walked into a room.

Gradually her kindness became known throughout the kingdom. Many even began to call her the "Good Princess."

Still, all this affirmation made Bonnie, the good fairy, edgy. People had quit calling her "Good Fairy" and were generally just calling her "The Fairy." One day, in fact, when Bonnie was trying to change a pumpkin into a coach, it only turned into a rutabaga. It took no genius to see what was abundantly clear: Bonnie was losing her powers as well as her reputation.

One day as Bonnie was walking along the street, she saw some children eating cookies.

"Where did you children get those cookies?" she asked.

"From the Good Dru-Ella," replied the children, "And just look at the nice doilies she crocheted. What's your name, lady?"

That did it!

Bonnie was furious and cast an evil spell on the house of Sturdley! The Good Dru-Ella fell asleep under the enchantment, and Bonnie made it very clear that Ms. Ugly would remain asleep until hell froze solid or some undiscriminating prince kissed her awake, which seemed highly unlikely to happen.

Meanwhile, on the other side of a huge mountain range far from Sturdley Castle, there lived Prince Gargoyle, who was so large of nose he had never been called "Prince Charming." Whenever he asked any maiden at the palace ball if she would like to dance, the girl would always say, "I'm sorry, I have arthritis!" But deep in his heart, Gargoyle knew the truth.

He was lonely, nasty, and ugly. Even people who were lonely, nasty, and ugly thought so. Still, all of his life he continued dreaming of meeting someone who would love him just for what he was . . . lonely, nasty, and ugly.

One day when he was feeling particularly ugly, he mounted his steed and rode off in search of adventure. He wandered for seven months, far across the mountains from his home. By oddest chance he happened to come upon a group of children who were wearing doilies for sun-caps. When they saw the prince, they said, "Yee-Gad!" which had now become the kingdom's common greeting. The homely prince was undaunted. He asked the children where they had gotten the lovely doilies they were wearing.

"From Sleeping Ugly," they explained. They told the prince that the princess was under a spell, and that while she was quite ugly, Gargoyle might want to consider kissing her awake. "There have been no cookies in the streets since the Good Dru-Ella fell under Bonnie's evil spell. Furthermore, there are no doilies either!" said one of the children.

"But Prince Gargoyle," warned another, "this will be no storybook romance! Dru-Ella Sturdley is not what you'd call beautiful. But on the other hand, Gargoyle, you're not exactly what people would call Prince Charm . . ." The child choked his near blunder into silence.

The Prince asked the way to the castle, and when he arrived there, Olaf showed him personally to the chamber of the comatose Dru-Ella. The prince asked him to leave the two of them alone. King Olaf withdrew, leaving only Prince Gargoyle and Sleeping Ugly together. Gargoyle studied her face for a long time. He had never kissed a girl before—even a comatose girl. He started to pucker and realized that puckering made him look even uglier, for when he puckered, the bristly wart on his upper lip grew as purple as the veins in his nose.

"Oh, never mind," he said as he unpuckered. He said to Sleeping Ugly, "My dearest Dru-Ella. They say that you are ugly, but I cannot believe it. I have seen children eating who once were hungry, and I know you gave them to eat. I have seen your lovely doilies, spun like golden spider fiber, glistening in the sun. It is not possible that one who reads to the blind and feeds the hungry could ever be ugly except to people who are so beautiful, they're vain."

He paused and studied her for a long time. "No, Dru-Ella, you are beautiful, and I hesitate to kiss you only because I am truly ugly, made so by selfishness and petty hatred. I shall draw my blade, and then I shall kiss you. If you wake and cry 'Yee-Gad!' then I shall slay myself. But if there is room in your good heart for one like me, then by God's good grace, I will love you for all eternity."

Prince Gargoyle repuckered and kissed her on the lips. (The instant he did, Bonnie—long cobwebbed-over in the dungeon of Sturdley Castle, felt a sharp pain in her neck. She knew her evil spell had been broken.) Sleeping Ugly awoke and, seeing Prince Gargoyle still puckered, she said, "Again, please!" This time Prince Gargoyle really kissed her—in a lingering, lippy lock-up. Their arms wound around each other in a desperate and clutching embrace. It was the longest kiss ever performed by those who rarely did it.

When the long, long kiss finally ended, Dru-Ella looked deeply into his eyes and said, "Gargoyle, my dear sweet prince, you've come. There is so much hurt in our kingdoms, my dearest, and I have discovered that when people are in real pain they do not even care about such words as 'pretty and ugly.' For true beauty is not made by strutting in front of mirrors.

"I have only two questions for you, Gargoyle. First, can you lay by your royal robes and come with me to help the poor, to tend the sick, and read to the blind?"

"My lovely Dru-Ella, you know I can!"

"Don't overdo the adjectives, Gargoyle. Just call me dear Dru-Ella! 'Lovely' is neither true nor necessary. My second question is a bit forward, but . . . will you marry me? There will be no photographers at the wedding. I couldn't stand having an album of pictures that no one ever asked to see."

"My dear Dru-Ella, here is my crown," said Gargoyle as he took it off and threw it on the floor. The clattering crown dropped out of sight and rolled through a huge grating. As the crown disappeared, the prince shouted, "I am free of you, you worthless old crown! You were always cold in the winter, and heavy all year long."

They were married.

Bonnie didn't go to the wedding.

Just as Dru-Ella expected, no one said, "What a fine looking couple you make!" Just as Gargoyle expected, nobody said, "What a lovely bride you have!"

But something new was loose in the kingdom. It was a spirit—a sense of true beauty.

Gargoyle and Dru-Ella honeymooned for two weeks in a leper colony, reading self-esteem books to lepers in the street. Cosmetic sales across the next few years dropped to zero, for all the people of the realm had found a way of life that was most beautiful and didn't depend on what one brushed on the face or stuck in the hair.

In time Dru-Ella and Gargoyle had children. As you would expect, heredity won out. Their children looked a lot like them, but the people of the kingdom simply called them the children of the king, for the words "ugly" and "pretty" were no longer in common usage. Even to this day, such words are not to be found in the dictionaries of that wonderful and happy land.

"Beauty is momentary in the mind—
The fitful tracing of a portal;
But in the flesh it is immortal.
The body dies; the body's beauty lives."
Wallace Stevens, *Peter Quince at the Clavier*

"When Jesus saw her, he called her forward and said to her, 'Woman, you are set free from your infirmity.'"
Luke 13:12

"Your beauty should not come from outward adornment, such as braided hair and the wearing of gold jewelry and fine clothes. Instead, it should be that of your inner self, the unfading beauty of a gentle and quiet spirit, which is of great worth in God's sight."
1 Peter 3:3-4

The Night the Sideshow Was Bought

We are all freaks in some way, I suppose. But let us not despair, for this has never mattered to Jesus, who bought the sideshow and set all of us free on one Good Friday long ago.

Myron/Myra, the hermaphrodite, was confused about who he/she was. Everyone else was also confused about themselves. Iva Gillette, the bearded lady, admitted from the very day she had joined the circus that she had been unable to see herself in any other way except as a freak! The word "freak" bothered Myron/Myra as much as it did Iva Gillette. Philip-Fido, the dog-faced boy, agreed. So did Thumbelina and the Fat Man.

The whole crew had been drawn into a common need for each other by terribly low self-esteem and the pittance of a salary which they all received just for being too fat or too little or too deformed. They had all endured years of being gawked at, laughed at, ogled, and despised.

None of them will ever forget the Thursday when their world seemed to perish. It was Thumbelina whose tiny voice broke into their odd gathering, "The circus is sold!"

"Who owns us now?" asked Philip-Fido.

"Oh, what difference does it make!" huffed the Fat Man, beginning to shake all over with sobs. His immense body rolled like a mountain under siege of a grievous earthquake. "We're freaks, freaks . . . freaks . . ." His voice trailed off.

Iva Gillette stroked her beard, then shook her head, and just sat there silently.

"Who owns us now?" Again Philip-Fido asked.

"I bought the circus," said a voice. The voice belonged to a tall, winsome man dressed in white.

He seemed kind, and the bearded lady smiled. "Whew, I was afraid our new owner would be just like the last one." Iva Gillette began to weep. "I wish my beard was pulled out."

"Mine was once," said the man in white.

Myron/Myra asked, "Who are you, and what do you know of being glowered at, laughed at, pointed at? Our last owner forced me to take off all my clothes every night so the ticket-holders could laugh at me."

"I was once naked and laughed at," said the man in white. They sat silent.

"I bought this sideshow so I could set you free," said the man in white. "You are bought! You are free!"

"Free?" said Thumbelina in tiny-voiced contempt. "You are tall and I am small. I am tired of being owned by anyone who's tall!"

"We are all small at times," said the man in white. "But human smallness is the invitation for God to act in a big way. You'd be surprised how small you feel when you're dwarfed by human hatred. Still you can trust me on this: "Small" is a state of heart that comes from having accepted too much of this world's harsh opinion. "Free" is getting the God-view of yourself. Trust me, you can be free. Indeed, you *shall* be free!"

"Free?" sneered the Fat Man.

"Free?" laughed Myron/Myra.

The man in white walked to the Fat Man, touched him, and he saw himself as a man of normal size. The Messiah then returned to Thumbelina, touched her, and she became tall. She cried, "Leave off the 'Thumbel'—I'm just 'Lena' now!" He also touched Philip-Fido, and his "dog-face" became lean and handsome. One touch and the bearded lady was suddenly beautiful of face.

"Which will it be? Myron or Myra?"

"Well, I've always liked baseball better than soap operas," he/she faltered.

"Very well—Myron!" said the man in white.

Instantly, Myron ordered Myra back to her daytime television, and she was gone forever. Myron felt whole, like a quarterback after a Rose Bowl touchdown!

Five very normal people at last watched while the man in white walked away. When he had reached a certain distance, he turned, took a Bic lighter, and flicked the flint wheel. Fire jumped from the wick, and he touched it to the canvas tent. He smiled. Amber canvas roared orange against the night.

"Speak no more of his renown.
Lay your earthly fancies down,
And in the vast cathedral leave him.
God accept him, Christ receive him."
Alfred, Lord Tennyson, *The Eagle*

"For God so loved the world that he gave his one and only Son, that whoever believes in him shall not perish but have eternal life."
John 3:16

"In that day they will say, 'Surely this is our God; we trusted in him, and he saved us. This is the LORD, we trusted in him; let us rejoice and be glad in his salvation.'"
Isaiah 25:9

Red Book, Blue Book

Christians have often set the mind at too great a distance from the heart. But the call to faith is more than a call to feel; it is also a call to know as much as we can. Faith needs not merely to be formed within us, but also to be informed by the world of books and insights.

Scarlett Redding was a reader. She was not just any old reader. She was a reader in search of excellence. Scarlett knew that excellence was somehow tied to the reading of books—good books—and so she read. Indeed, she read regularly, often stopping only to change books or replace the bulb in her desk lamp. She had not read all of the books there were, for she was born into the age of books. And all books were as red in color as the blushing librarians who collected all her overdue fines.

It was odd! There was no law which said that all books had to be red in color; that's just the way it was. So if you were a reader, all of your reading was done from red books.

They were not all the same shade of red. Some were catsup red, some were rose red, some were Tabasco, others were strawberry popsicle. There were light red books and deep red books. Serious books were crimson, while books that didn't need to be taken so seriously were barely pink.

Scarlett's room was lined with books, and thus it was ringed with red. Indeed, her own little room was nearly as red as the inside of a bookstore, which was the reddest place known to the human race. But Scarlett began to find as she grew older that red no longer intrigued her. Red went dead for Scarlett. She found herself becoming disconsolate. Pink, cerise, and crimson all spelled "bore." Finally she quit reading alto-gether. When she passed the red windows of bookstores, she always looked the other way.

The colorless, bookless months passed Scarlett by.

One day as Scarlett passed a bookstore, an old man extended his hand to her and beckoned her inside. She fol-lowed. The red interior gave her hot flashes as she passed the boring shelves and entered the back room. In the room at the back of the store, the old man handed her a plain brown bag and told her not to open it until she was safely at home!

She obeyed. Then suddenly, Scarlett froze. Maybe he was an Episcopalian! Her mother had always told her to avoid Episcopalians with brown bags. She hurried out of the store and, clutching her little brown bag, hurried through the streets. She could not imagine what was in the bag, but she guarded it as though some lurking fiend might leap out from behind a shrub and tear it forcibly away.

At last she arrived home. Eagerly her hands tore away the paper sack, and there greeted her a most wonderful sight—a blue book! How odd this was! She felt as though she was doing something terribly wrong, just to hold a book so blue. "I'll bet he *was* an Episcopalian," thought Scarlett. "No sin-cere Baptist would read a blue book." Still, she could not be critical for long. The blue of the book hypnotized her. It was banner blue and robin's egg blue. It was jay blue and sea blue and star blue. It was a frothy waterfall in summer. It was lying-flat-on-the-grass-and-looking-up-at-the-sky-all-alone-in-July blue.

Scarlett clutched the book to her bosom and looked around. The red books in her room seemed to glare in disapproval. So she turned her back on the glaring, haughty books and flexed the bright blue cover of her new book nervously in her fingers. In a trembling fashion she cautiously opened the cover, and the book read in rainbow letters, *A Truly Excellent Book*.

"What would a truly excellent book contain?" wondered Scarlett as she turned to the table of contents. She was surprised that there were only three chapters. The first chapter was called "God Is All Over." The second chapter was called "God Has a Boy Just Like Us." The third chapter was titled "The World Is Wide and There Are Many Kinds of Truth."

Scarlett turned to Chapter One. And when she rubbed her finger over the words "God Is All Over," she felt altogether weak with wonder. For no sooner had her finger touched the word "God" than her eyes beheld a thousand scenes of stars and galaxies and lands. There were colliding sun-systems that kept exploding so brightly that Scarlett was struck silent by the laser majesty that ripped her room with light.

"Oh, this *is* an excellent book!" she said. "Never did I know that God is all over till right now."

She turned to Chapter Two: "God Has a Boy Just Like Us." This was the very best chapter she had ever read, for never had she seen the wonder of being alive until that moment. She saw God's boy! He was handsome and kind and very strong. God's boy was just like God. "God's boy is God's show-and-tell," said Scarlett half-aloud. "Still, he's not only like God; he's like me too!" She could tell just by looking at him that there was nothing he couldn't do, and yet he was just like her. It made her feel good to know that God had a boy just like her, for she knew that God's boy understood just how good it felt to feel good and how bad it felt to feel bad.

"Maybe old Episcopalians aren't all that bad," thought Scarlett. Then she read the title of Chapter Three.

It was this third chapter that gave her so much trouble. It didn't seem related to the first and second chapters. She thought and thought about the title of the third chapter: "The World Is Wide and There Are Many Kinds of Truth."

She thought about all the kinds of truth that didn't seem very related to God at all. She thought of trigonometry and microwave makers and cosmetology and peanut butter factories; she thought of silver nitrate and cave paintings and Egg McMuffins and submarines and curling irons and suspension bridges and malt balls and tenant farmers and astronauts and Disney World and leg warmers and George Washington. How did all of these kinds of truth relate? She simply couldn't understand. "Yes, there are many kinds of truth that don't seem related to God at all," she thought.

"This book on excellence is hard. To be excellent you have to think too hard," she thought. "The World Is Wide and There Are Many Kinds of Truth." Scarlett kept thinking about that last chapter until at last she fell sound asleep.

In the morning, the very first thing that Scarlett reached for was her new blue book. She read. When she came again to the troublesome third chapter, no matter how hard she tried, she just couldn't make it relate to the others. This made her very sad. "Episcopalian blue—that's what this book is," she thought. "I shouldn't read blue books; they only confuse me, for there is too much truth in the world . . . no, that's absurd. There could never be too much truth, only too many lies."

As Scarlett got dressed for the day, perplexed by these unsettling thoughts, she had an idea. She walked down Third

Street to Lincoln Avenue, past her church to the public library. The library had always been there, right next to the church, but Scarlett rarely went there. The truth is that red evangelicals hardly had time for libraries. They were at church a lot. Theirs was a world of glo-red revival meetings and reeking red renewal weekends. There were prayer services and Revelation studies. There were film series, red-red committee alerts, and program planning sessions for all the meetings. So the red people hardly had time for libraries.

But now Scarlett walked into the library and saw that the entire building was filled with books. Just as she expected, the books were mostly red and various shades of red, except that here and there she could see a blue book. The blue books seemed like they were all friends, even though they were usually a long ways apart on the shelves.

"The world really is big," thought Scarlett, "and there are many kinds of truth." Scarlett turned down an aisle between huge ranks of books. The shelves stretched up so high above her, she had to get a ladder to reach the top. She got a big ladder and shoved it to the top of a section called ANATOMY. Scarlett climbed all the way to the top, and there she pulled out a little blue book. It was titled *Human Anatomy*.

She opened the book. On one of the pages was a picture of a skeleton. "I must have a skeleton inside of me, too!" said Scarlett. And then it occurred to her that if God's boy was just like her, he must have had a skeleton inside him too. On the skeleton's leg was a word that read *femur*.

"I have a femur," thought Scarlett, "and I guess if I have one, God's boy must have had a femur too." It made her feel silly thinking about Jesus' femur, but she was sure it must be true.

She thumbed on through the pages till she saw another picture of a man with his skin gone away. He was all muscles, and each of his muscles was labeled with little black lines that ran from his muscles out to a big, long word. She saw one muscle called *biceps femoris*. She said the word out loud. "BI-CEPS FE-MORIS." (Scarlett had found that difficult words had to be sounded out loud to be pronounced.) Several people who were nearby shushed her, since they did not like to hear anyone say "biceps femoris" out loud in the library.

"Hmm, I must have a biceps femoris too . . . and so did God's boy. The world is wide and there are many kinds of truth." Suddenly she could see that God was all through the library.

All day long she stayed in the library. She read a book about mushrooms and could see that God's truth was all through the book. Even those people who cultivated mushrooms were just like God's boy.

"That's funny," said Scarlett, "even books that ignore God have some truth in them." She felt sorry for people who didn't believe in God, but it made her feel very good that even their books had many truths in them. "Truth doesn't have to be *about* God to be *friends* with God," she thought.

At the top of one of the shelves, Scarlett saw a book with the title *Gravity*. It was a book that told the truth about how nobody could float up and away and off the earth. Scarlett was happy for that truth. For gravity held her to the floor of the library. It also once held God's boy to the ground. Scarlett, knowing that she could barely make good *gravy*, was especially grateful that God could make gravity. "It's just like God to keep our feet flat on the ground while we learn all about him," thought Scarlett.

When Scarlett went home that night, she saw for the first time that there was much to be found alike between all three chapters of her new blue book. She loved it. She read it every day and every night. And every new fact that Scarlett heard, she tried to think, "Is this book the truth? And how is it related to the truth that God is all over and had a boy just like me?"

Sunday finally came and Scarlett went to church. Scarlett just loved her little red church, for they always had a place right at the very end of the service where you could tell something "wonderful and glorious" you had learned that week. It was called "wonderful and glorious time."

The preacher preached a wonderful sermon entitled "God Is All Over." Scarlett thought of her new blue book and was very happy. When the preacher finished, the choir sang a glorious anthem called "God Has a Boy Just Like Us." Scarlett smiled.

When the choir was finished, it was "wonderful and glorious time," and the preacher asked if anyone had learned anything new that week.

"Yes," cried Scarlett, "I learned that the world is wide and there are many kinds of truth."

Everyone looked very embarrassed. Finally the preacher cleared his throat and said, "Is this fact related to 'God is all over'? You know how we feel here; it must be related."

"Yes, I think so. For the more I read at the library . . ."

An old woman in the choir stiffened, "The library, HUMPH!" She cupped her hand over her mouth and whispered to a bony-faced man beside her, "You can learn some bad truths in the library."

"Oh no!" cried Scarlett. "There are no bad truths . . . that's another thing I've learned this week. All truths are the friends of God."

"Why didn't you come to the all-red revival and renewal retreat?" rasped the old woman. "If you want to live a red and righteous life, you must keep away from blue books."

One man gasped! He had never heard anyone say "blue books" right in church! "Is that all you learned this week, little girl . . . that the world is wide and there are many kinds of truth?"

"Oh, no," cried Scarlett, "I learned that Jesus had a femur and a biceps femoris."

Now everybody gasped!

"Enough!" they cried. Just then someone noticed that Scarlett was carrying a blue book. A strong elder tore it from her hand and took it to the pastor. "Burn it," he cried.

"Please, no!" cried Scarlett. But they took the book away, and Scarlett cried all the way home. Could she have been mistaken? *Was the world not wide? Were there not many kinds of truth?*

When morning came, she got up and got dressed, and decided that she would give up books and church forever. She shuffled along the sidewalks, going nowhere in particular, when she saw an old man with a brown sack under his arm. "Uh-oh," she thought, "it's that same, wonderful old Episcopalian."

She hid behind a row of shrubs, and the old man sauntered past her. He was mumbling something. She listened very carefully. He was old, and she hated to hear him talking to himself, for she felt like she was eavesdropping. Yet she had a strange inclination to follow him.

Quickly Scarlett stepped behind the old man and trailed along after him. He never saw her, but she kept her eyes on him and particularly the brown sack he carried. She thought she knew what was in it.

At last the old man turned into a shady lane and walked down a path through the row of trees. There was a little white house at the side of the road. On the door of the little white house was a sign: "ENTER HERE WITH A WORD OF TRUTH." The old man turned toward the door and raised the brass lion's head that served as the door knocker. He rapped three times and the door opened just a little. Someone on the inside said, "The password please!"

"The world is wide and there are many kinds of truth," said the old man, too softly for Scarlett to hear.

How Scarlett wished she could hear what he had said, but once he was inside, she knew she had to get into that little house too. Quickly she ran up to the door and knocked with the great lion's head knocker three times. The door creaked open only a little on its hinges. "Yes?" said a throaty voice.

"May I come in?" asked Scarlett.

"You may enter with a word of truth," said someone inside.

I wonder what kind of truth he wants, thought Scarlett. She knew she would have to guess. "Mt. Everest is the highest mountain on earth."

The door slammed! Scarlett rapped again.

Again the door creaked open, and the man inside insisted this time, "You may enter only with a word of truth."

Scarlett was desperate! "Jupiter is the largest planet in the solar system," she blurted.

Again the door slammed shut.

Scarlett was confused. Maybe just any old truth wasn't good enough for the doorkeeper. Maybe the password should try to relate truths of all kinds to certain specific truths. It was worth a try, so she rapped the lion's head the third time.

The door swung open only an inch or so.

"Password, please," said the throaty voice.

"Jesus had a femur and a biceps femoris." Scarlett felt ashamed. There were so many kinds of truth, but she couldn't think of any of them that was great enough to impress the doorkeeper. She fully expected the door to slam shut.

"Well, it isn't exactly the truth we were looking for," he said, "but it is a truth that does relate to the fact that God is all over and God had a boy. I guess we'll have to let you in. Have you ever read a blue book?"

"I had one once, but I lost it in church."

"During wonderful and glorious time?" asked the door-keeper.

Scarlett was amazed, and even as her mouth dropped open, she entered the room. It was filled with many people, and all of them had blue books. There were paper sacks all over the floor.

"Do you love God?" they asked Scarlett.

"Oh yes!" said Scarlett.

"Do you believe he is all over?"

"Not only all over, but all over all over!"

Scarlett felt that she was overdoing it now.

"Do you believe he had a boy just like us?"

"Oh yes . . . not only just like us, but just like all the people who read only red books or no books at all. His boy was like every person that ever lived . . . like the men and like the little children and like the poor people who starve to death and like scientists who sometimes teach things we don't believe and like people from Indiana and astronauts and . . ."

The man who asked the question cleared his throat. "Do you truly believe that Jesus was God's boy and had a femur and a biceps femoris? Are you willing to take a stand for all truth . . . even during wonderful and glorious time?"

"Oh, yes sir, for the world is big and there are many kinds of truth."

"Then you are welcome."

A little man advanced from the side and handed her a blue book of her own.

"Treasure this book," he said, "for such books are owned by those who really care about true excellence."

"Are there many alive right now in our world who care about excellence?" asked Scarlett.

"There have never been many who care about excellence," said the little man, "but numbers don't matter, my dear Scarlett. Only excellence matters."

"Now," he said, "let us all take out our books."

And they all did. First they turned to Chapter One. They all felt the words "God is All Over." The room darkened and a bright light traveled in an orbit around a growing universe. It was wonderful and glorious, but Scarlett knew it was wider and better than that.

Then they turned to Chapter Two and felt the words "God Has a Boy Just Like Us." As they rubbed the words, the great light in the center of the center of the universe condensed down and became a man—a handsome man—and Scarlett could see that he was maltreated. She couldn't see a book in his hand, but it was almost as though they had torn a blue book away from him and had nailed him on a tree. And he cried out some words. Scarlett couldn't tell what the words were, but it must have sounded like the password, for the heavens opened a little way and then soon he was dead.

But then he was alive again! Then Scarlett saw a wonderful thing. God's boy began to rise off a mountaintop and floated upward. "Books on gravity teach that rising upward is impossible," remembered Scarlett. "Oh well, I guess if God makes gravity, he can unmake it whenever he wants to!"

Soon the meeting was over, and all of the people put their blue books back into their sacks and left the quiet little house of wonders. Scarlett walked home alone past the library and smiled at all the truth it contained. Then she walked past the church and thought of all the truth it contained. And she clutched her little paper sack and knew that libraries and churches didn't have to be afraid of each other ever again.

She hopped off the ground and tried to imagine how Jesus felt the day he made gravity look silly. But she was glad inside. And she thought of Jesus and smiled. Wasn't it like him to love Episcopalians and ordinary mushroom pickers who needed gravity to keep them hanging around?

"Thank you, Jesus, for being just like us," she said out loud. It was a beautiful day.

She felt good, too—all the way down to her femur and her biceps femoris.

(Knowledge) is a rich storehouse for the glory of the Creator and the relief of man's estate."
Frances Bacon, *The Advancement of Learning*

"He who is not with me is against me, and he who does not gather with me scatters."
Matthew 12:30

"A man who lacks judgment derides his neighbor,
but a man of understanding holds his tongue."
Proverbs 11:12

Section 5

Frying Rabbits

Putting Jesus Back into the Calendar

Frying Rabbits

Notes for secular Resurrectionists

Once upon a time, at that very time of year when it was known for a fact that a dead carpenter rose from the dead, a very pretty Celtic goddess named Oeästre (pronounced *ay-AHS-tray*) was seen tripping through the woods, hiding colored eggs in the deep, dark, druid forests of ancient Angle Terra, about three fortnights of bunny-hopping east of Stonehenge.

Well, it happened, that Peter Cottontail, brother to Flopsy, Mopsy, and Hopsy, was in the forest at that very time, and approached Oeästre saying, "Eggs? Eggs? What can this mean?"

"It means," said Oeästre, "that spring hath sprung! It means, dear hare-brained rabbit, that fertility has come. The earth is being reborn. Eggs, you see, are symbols of fertility— of life—of nature and freshness."

"Eggs," said Peter, "also make nice omelets when scrambled into cheese and carrots."

"Not these eggs. These eggs have been boiled and colored," said Oeästre.

"Well, it seems to me," objected Peter, "that celebrating eggs could confuse people who like to use this time of year to think about you-know-who, who rose from the dead."

"Don't you mention his name in my presence! My religion is a very private thing!"

"Okay! But don't you think people might get confused and get even these colored eggs all scrambled together with pagan fertility rituals?"

"Well, then, we'll call them Easter eggs . . . silly rabbit."

"But won't these eggs tend to steal dignity from the miracle of the Resurrection?" asked the rabbit.

"Not necessarily. We'll write 'He Is Risen' on some of the sacred blue eggs and 'He's Alive' on some of the yellow eggs."

"But won't that be wrong?"

"Well, tell me this, bucky teeth, how else are we gonna get the fertility season into department stores? If you think these national department stores are gonna put up pictures of you-know-who coming out of a tomb over the racks of new frocks, you're wrong! Besides, my idea is a perfect example of verbal economy. 'Happy Resurrection Sunday' has eight syllables. 'Happy Easter' only four."

"Yeah, but . . ."

Peter's words were choked to silence as Oeästre reached down and pinched his little mouth closed around his buck teeth.

"Mmmmph" said Peter, trying to say, "I'm going to expose you, Oeästre, to the vice squad!" But he could not talk very well with his mouth pinched shut.

Therefore, the exposure he might have made to get the record straight never came to be. So Oeästre's cunning deception was prevented from ever being discovered. How?

Well, that night, after hiding eggs all over the woods, Oeästre dined on fried rabbit. And after picking her teeth and flossing, she dialed the Cottontail residence. The phone rang three times before Oeästre heard a tiny click of the receiver.

"Hello," said an innocent naïve doe.

"Flopsy?" asked Oeästre.

"Mopsy!"

"Oh, Mopsy. Mopsy, dear, this is Oeästre."

"Oh, hello. Say, have you seen our brother, Peter? He's not home yet."

"No, I hope you find him. He's a bunny of exquisite taste . . . but Mopsy, deary, the reason I called is that I would like to make you three girls poster rabbits for the Resurrection season. Interested?"

"You mean like we'd be famous every spring?"

"In every department store in the world, I guarantee it."

Well, that's how it all started. Three rather plain bunnies who had never been praised for their natural beauty become famous overnight. Oeästre told everyone that the bunnies had laid the colored eggs. Even though no one really believed her, the idea caught on.

And so it happened that Flopsy, Mopsy and Hopsy, in a few short years became nationwide symbols of fertility and springtime. Peter was silent, having been fried. Too bad, for he might have blown the whistle on the entire cover-up.

But rabbits can't come back from the dead you know.

"An egg is dear on Easter Day."
Anonymous Russian proverb

"Jesus answered them, 'Destroy the temple, and I will raise it again in three days.'"
John 2:19

"We have testified about God that he raised Christ from the dead. But he did not raise him if in fact the dead are not raised. For if the dead are not raised, then Christ has not been raised either. And if Christ has not been raised, your faith is futile; you are still in your sins."
1 Corinthians 15:15-17

The North Pole Apology

Santa has a habit of ignoring those who have been naughty or nice . . . in favor of those who are richer or poorer.

I wanted to write an apology to you kids who aren't getting anything this Christmas. I know some of you have been waiting for several Christmases for me to stop by, and you must be disappointed that I haven't been showing up.

The truth is, it has nothing to do with whether you have a chimney or not. Oh, to be sure, I do prefer nice, wide chimneys, but I can work around the hazards presented by tighter entrances. Furnace flues and vent pipes, back doors and transoms: all serve very well.

It also has nothing to do with whether or not you live in mobile homes. My reindeer can land very lightly on tin roofs and never cave one in. In fact, I can land the old sleigh just about anywhere.

It really has nothing to do with whether you've been naughty or nice. A lot of you have been nearly sinless and have still not gotten a present in years.

It's mostly a matter of reality and expectation.

It hurts me to say this, but rich kids are more demanding. Can you see why all of you poor kids haven't been getting anything for years? You are too realistic and have very low expectations. But this is not true across town where the rich kids live. They have very high expectations, so if they order a video machine and their own television, I feel something of an obligation to them. They get so mad when they don't get everything they ask for. I get the nastiest letters on the twenty-sixth of December from rich little kids who ask for so many things I can hardly remember them all.

Let me read you a letter from Jimmy of Knickerbocker Hills:

Dear Santa:

You are a real loser! Where's the three-ton gift package of Legos that I ordered? I told you three times at Macy's what I wanted. What a schmuck! I couldn't believe it when I got up on Christmas morning, and all I had was the two-ton package. Now I won't be able to build my replica of the Empire State Building like I was planning. I suppose I'll just have to wait till next Christmas. But no more milk and cookies for you, Buster. And if you see the Easter Bunny, tell him that in my April basket, I want more chocolate eggs and fewer marshmallow "peeps."

Sincerely,
Jimmy of Knickerbocker Hills

P.S. You forgot the bell on the bike you brought me, you fat, red buffoon.

Would you believe I've got to respond to a legal complaint from a seven-year-old in Marin County who is suing me for breach of promise—a promise I made in the Ghiardelli Square in October? I forgot her Barbie Convertible, she says. The truth is, I brought her one the previous Christmas, and Ken wrecked it in a head-on collision with G.I. Joe's tank. But gift supply here at the North Pole was low on Barbie Convertibles last year, so I figured she could wait till next Christmas. She's contesting my decision in court.

So, you see, I am kept so busy with hate mail and litigations that I just haven't had the time to get around to all of you poor kids. But you are so nice, you never write me those kinds of letters. When I make you a promise in the Wal-Mart, you never really take me seriously. It helps on Christmas Eve, when I'm trying to get around to everyone, to know that if I have to miss you, you won't get upset or anything.

Maybe you poor kids should organize. Bring some pressure on the North Pole and force my hand. It helped four years ago in one of the ghettos. Seven poor kids got together and formed the PKFKSS (Poor Kids for Keeping Santa Straight). They lobbied with the Newark courts and filed a petition for Equal Yuletide Treatment. Naturally I had to respond or look politically insensitive. So, the next Christmas, I can tell you I dumped a lot of junk down those chimneys.

But there sure a lot of you poor little kids, so don't expect a miracle.

Jesus of Nazareth is really a better bet than I am. He loves everybody and never leaves anybody out. I don't see how he does it, though. Maybe it helps when you're the Son of God and don't have a lot of reindeer to take care of. If I were you, I'd keep in touch with Jesus. After all, Christmas is his birthday and he can do so much more for you than I can.

He's always been a better bet for all kids. He never forgets anybody.

This will be really important as you get older. There will come a time when my elves and I won't be able to do much for you. It's then that Jesus really shines.

Frankly, he makes me feel ashamed that I always treat the rich better than the poor. I'm embarrassed to admit it, but I've always been pretty upper class.

Not him, though. He was born poor. He doesn't give gifts; he *is* the gift!

Take it from old Santa.

Merrily Yours,
Santa Claus
The North Pole

"Nobody shoots at Santa Claus."
Alfred Emanuel Smith, *Campaign Speeches*

"Let the little children come to me, and do not hinder them, for the kingdom of heaven belongs to such as these."
Matthew 19:14

"Thanks be to God for his indescribable gift."
2 Corinthians 9:15

The Old 100th Revisited Yet Again

Inspired by "A Thanksgiving Litany" by Joan Beck.

Make a joyful noise unto the Lord, all ye lands!

Give thanks to Him!
For the beauty of the earth, for the glory of the skies,
For the love that, from our birth, over and around us lies.
Give thanks, till your benedictions
Celebrate His benevolence . . .

Till your prayers celebrate His purposes,
    till your hallelujahs celebrate His holiness,
    till your glorias glorify Him,
    till your magnificats magnify Him.
Give thanks till your oblations are your obsessions,
    till gratitude is your attitude.
Give thanks to Him till foolish self-sufficiency is erased,
    and glorious self-denial is enhanced.
Give thanks till you see the grace of His abundance,
    as the cornucopia of His harvest,
    spilling from your meager seedtimes.
Give thanks—
    for joys immeasurable and full of glory!
    for pain unhealable and full of humanity!
    for shame unanswerable and full of humility!
    for grief unbearable and filled with the presence of God!

for despair that ends in hope,
for tears that end in laughter,
for failure that brings us as low as we could ever go,
so that we can ascend to heights that are
unimaginable from the depths.
Give thanks for the children, the charities,
the choices you have, yes,
even for charlatans and cheeky achievers,
for cheers and chats and chants,
and chips and chunks of chocolate.

Serve the Lord with gladness!
Give thanks to Him!

Come ye thankful people, come,
raise the song of harvest home!
All is safely gathered in, ere the winter storms begin.

In all things, give thanks.
For all things, give thanks.
Give thanks regardless.
Thank Him for beauty spots,
which He makes from common moles and warts.
Thank Him for the little itches
that in the scratching makes your nails stronger.
Thank Him for the bird calls,
the house calls, the phone calls,
The computer calls,
the crank calls, the kid's calls.
Thank Him for the foods you don't like
and people you don't like,

For broccoli and Hefner, and spinach and Lewinski,
For anchovies and Darth Vader,
   for Slobodan Milosovich and *Green Eggs and Ham*.

Thank Him for bothersome, dull television commercials,
   and you will know you are truly a person of good will.

Thank Him for your income tax,
   and you will know you are truly grateful to live in America.

Thank him for the house calls of Jehovah's Witnesses,
   and you will know you are truly free from prejudice.

Thank Him for Republicans if you're a Democrat,
   and for Democrats if you're a Republican.

Thank Him for your weaknesses
   that keep you ever turning to Him for strength.

Thank the Lord!

Come before His presence with singing!

Every need His hand supplying, every good in Him I see.
On His strength divine relying, He is all in all to me!

Sing like Caruso, like an angel, like a frog!
Like a monotone, a quadrophone,
   a gramophone, a megaphone.
Sing like the Brooklyn Tabernacle Choir,
   the Vienna Boys Choir,

the St. Olaf's Choir, the Senior Singers,
the Oak Ridge boys, the Florida Boys, the Beach Boys,
like Elvis, like Garth, like Patti—but sing!

Sing your doctrine!
Sing that the Lord, He is God.
Sing that it is He that has made us in His image.

Now thank we all our God, with heart and hand and voices.
Who wondrous things has done, in whom His world rejoices!

It is God who makes bad people good,
     who makes good people better,
     who makes goody, goody people possible to live with.

He has made us! Sing to the Lord!
We are fearfully and wonderfully made!
We have arteries and ovaries,
     pituitaries, pulmonaries, and ears.
We have muscles and vessels and tonsils
     and auricles and ventricles and mandibles
     and follicles, umbilicals, and vesicles!
It is He that hath made us and not we ourselves.
So sing to the Lord!

We are His people and the sheep of His pasture!

Give thanks for your sheephood!
Oh, bless His name!
He is our Shepherd; He leads us in paths of righteousness!
Give thanks for His leadership.

He leads us beside the still waters!
Give thanks for the waters!
He restoreth our souls.
Give thanks for the restoration!
We are His people! We have His blessings!
We have the blessing of peace, of prosperity,
    of poise, of personality, of privacy,
    of penance, of profit, persistence,
    perseverance, and position in Christ.
Praise His name, He is ours! Rejoice, all things are ours!
Salvation, sanctification, satisfaction.
All things are ours!
Menthol, Protocol, Cepacol, ethanol, alcohol.

Enter His gates with thanksgiving!
Come into His courts with praise!

We gather together to ask the Lord's blessings,
He chastens and hastens His will to make known;
Ordaining, maintaining His kingdom divine.

In His Kingdom are His promises.
In His Kingdom is our destiny.
In His Kingdom are our bread, our broth,
    our breath, our brotherhood,
    our brass ring, our brazen serpent of salvation.
Give thanks to Him and praise His name,
For the Lord is good and His love endures forever,
His faithfulness continues through all generations.

"The day thou gavest, Lord, is ended,
The darkness falls at thy behest;
To thee our morning hymns ascended,
Thy praise shall sanctify our rest."
John Ellerton, *Hymn*

"The shepherds returned, glorifying and praising God for all the things they had heard and seen, which were just as they had been told."
Luke 2:20

"Therefore in the east give glory to the Lord; exalt the name of the Lord, the God of Israel, in the islands of the sea."
Isaiah 24:15

A Shepherd's Testimony

In December of 1992, a group of students was putting on a mini-pageant for our seminary. One of them asked me why it was that the shepherds never got any good lines in Christmas pageants. I reminded him that shepherds were part of the working class, but that the kings were the wealthy sponsors of the Nativity. After I thought it over, however, I decided that here and there, at least in some pageants, it would be all right for the shepherds to get some time. So I wrote this little piece to give shepherds a place in the program. After all, Nativity stories should be places where even the blue-collared folks get their turn.

It was just after midnight when the gold broke all around us! The light stung my eyes. It was the worst I've ever felt, I tell you. I choked and gagged. I don't know why—I must have been allergic to all that light.

I was terrified. These big, silvery white beings belched out of the skies, like a tangled flock of big geese. Tall as Mount Hermon and big as Philistines. Those big, bright fellows exploded out of the shattered blackness and fell like the sparks from the blacksmith's forge all around our feet. The sheep whelped like wolf cubs and hid their little black faces in each other's fleeces.

I turned to see how my fellow shepherds were doing. My friend Ben was worse off than I was. He was lying on the ground in a stone-cold faint.

Judah was still conscious, but he had his face hidden in his sleeve, muttering, "No, no . . . no!" My skin started to crawl.

My eyes twitched. The hair on my neck prickled and then tried to crawl down my collar.

Name any fear I've ever felt before this, and I'll deny the force of it. I never in all my life was afraid till that night. The angels did it all. They burst upon me, forcing me into the sheer terror of seeing that much splendor at midnight. It was like the dark nightmares you have as a child, but it was a nightmare with all light. I saw everything, and I trembled.

"Fear not!" said one of the big fellows. (His message was half a coronary too late for Ben.) "I bring you good news! A baby's been born. 'This day in the city of David, a Savior. . . . And this shall be a sign unto you: you shall find the baby wrapped in clean cloths and lying in a manger.'"

This, I assume, was the way angels asked you to set out looking for stuff.

The light was still eye-painful and bright, but I didn't have the nerve to say, "Please call off this light, would you?" All of a sudden the whole flock—or whatever you call a group of angels—started singing, "Glory to God in the highest and on earth, peace to men of good will!"

Then they were gone, just like that!

When all that light and noise was over, things got dark and quiet. The dark was so dark you couldn't see your hand in front of your face.

"You still there, Judah?" I whispered, still recovering from the whole thing. No answer.

"Judah," I spoke a little louder now, "are you there?"

"For pity's sake, be quiet. They might come back!" he said.

"Think we ought to do what they said and go look for the baby? Can we leave the sheep out here without one of us?"

"They're not going anywhere; they're too paralyzed to

move." About this time Ben regained consciousness, and after we explained everything about the light and the angels and the whole chorus, the three of us started off toward Bethlehem.

Our legs were all goose bumps during the first mile of our walk into Bethlehem. And we got off to a slow start because our knees were knocking. But gradually we settled into a faster pace.

We found the tiny baby and his folks just like the angels said. I don't know why this surprised us. There they were, and the baby was wrapped in clean cloths and lying in a manger.

We didn't feel too comfortable barging in on the little family. And even though there was something kingly and queenly about the mother and father, they weren't dressed much better than Ben, Judah, and I were. But it seemed the right thing to do, somehow . . . just falling on our knees.

We didn't know what to say to the new parents. Judah said, "Congratulations on your new kid; the angels told us about him."

Then Ben said, "You must have been pregnant a long time." It was the stupidest thing I ever heard anybody say. Judah elbowed him in the ribs for being so mutton-headed. Ben hardly ever left the sheep, so he never had developed much in the way of social graces. I guess it seemed logical to him.

The woman just smiled, to let him know he could be an idiot if he liked. I kind of glossed the whole thing over by saying, "There must be something really special about your little baby, if angels are having a big party for him in the fields at night."

Long after we got up off our knees and went back to the sheep, I kept thinking about that evening. I never will forget two things about that night: I'll never forget Ben's stupidity, and I'll never forget how beautiful that couple looked. They were peasants, I guess. Still, I've never quit wondering who they were and who their baby grew up to be.

And one other thing I've never gotten over: I just never have trusted the dark again. Ever since that night, I get a little edgy around midnight.

[The shepherds who launched Christmas were humble.] "Not only humble but 'umble, which I look upon to be the comparative, or indeed, superlative degree."
Anthony Trollope, *Doctor Thorne*

"In those days Caesar Augustus issued a decree that a census should be taken of the entire Roman world. (This was the first census that took place while Quirinius was governor of Syria.) And everyone went to his own town to register. So Joseph also went up from the town of Nazareth in Galilee to Judea, to Bethlehem the town of David, because he belonged to the house and line of David. He went there to register with Mary, who was pledged to be married to him and was expecting a child. While they were there, the time came for the baby to be born, and she gave birth to her firstborn, a son. She wrapped him in cloths and placed him in a manger, because there was no room for them in the inn."
Luke 2:1-7

"But when the time was fully come, God sent his Son, born of a woman, born under law."
Galatians 4:4

Section 6

X-Rated Muffins

Christ and Sexual Sanity

The Muffin Man

In a world of indulgence, self-control is an act of love, given as a present to the Lord of the seventh commandment.

Murray was fourteen before he really began to notice muffins. He was seventeen when they became a roaring issue in his life. His compulsion for muffins came upon him all at once in late adolescence. All at once his whole world seemed to center around them. It wasn't just bakeries that tempted him, either. Everyone sold muffins: cafes and restaurants, bars and service stations.

It was Madison Avenue that really went berserk. Muffins were used to sell everything from cologne to carburetors. Murray saw huge billboards that said, "Fly Acapulco," and sure enough, right there on the billboard would be a picture of a muffin.

The muffins always looked good! Many books had muffins somewhere in the dust-jacket photos. And you didn't have to read any novel very far before the hero and heroine sat down to huge helpings of muffins. The more they ate, the better the book sold. Those that were best sellers had muffins eaten on every page, usually in fits of desperate mouth-cramming and lots of choking noises.

Muffins even factored into the way theaters rated their films. Certain letters would mean things like, "See 101 Black-spotted Dogs Approved for Children—No Muffins." Others said "No Kids Allowed—Muffins in Every Scene."

Murray would have gone on living with a muffin-saturated

world except that he went to church. The preacher would say, "Keep away from all this godless muffinizing. Yes, brothers and sisters—bran, blueberry, rye, raisin, or raw cocoa: all are depraved." He'd often end his sermon with the story of a beautiful young girl who laid down her Bible and fell into a life of dissipating muffinizing that led her at last to the gutters of gluttony.

On Sundays, Murray listened and agreed to avoid the epidemic of muffin mania that was sweeping the country. But on Mondays it was harder to carry out his resolution. "After all," he said to himself, "I'm young, and muffins are the singular preoccupation of the young. What's a guy gonna do?"

One Friday he went to the gym and shot a few baskets. While dressing, he heard the guys talking about the weekend muffins they were going to eye. He knew they'd meet again on Monday, and the muffin report would come in.

Murray, too, had a date set up for that evening. Her name was Helen. She was beautiful. In merely thinking of her, muffin mania settled down upon Murray.

On the night of the date, he took her to a movie. There were plenty of muffins in it. He took her out for dessert, and beads of perspiration broke out all over him. "Helen," he said as they drove up to her house, "about muffins . . ." He looked at her hopefully, but she was intractable!

"Murray," she said, "Those who eat dessert first spoil the banquet of life. Never think of muffins before dinner. Never say, 'I want' before 'I do.' Muffins are incredibly good, but never out of season."

They kissed goodnight. They dated again and again. Murray usually thought about muffins the entire time he was with Helen, but he never said so.

After a courtship of two years, Murray took her to the altar. Murray kissed her after they played "Trumpet Voluntary" and "O Promise Me." They cut the cake and drank punch. They opened gifts and flew away to Niagara Falls.

He carried her across the threshold of their motel room. He was jubilant. "Yahoo!" he shouted, "Muffins at last!" They never spoke of muffins in public, but if ever a couple could be said to know the contentment and fullness of muffins, it was Murray and Helen. To everything there is a season, of course, and those who wait to bless their bread know that muffins are far too rich to speak of in the shallow company of gluttons who devour the dough because the oven takes too long.

"So we think of Marilyn who was every man's love affair with America, Marilyn Monroe who was blond and beautiful and had a sweet little rinky-dink of a voice and all the cleanliness of all the clean American backyards. She was our angel, the sweet angel of sex, and the sugar of sex came up from her like a resonance of sound in the clearest grain of a violin."
Norman Mailer, *Marilyn*

"But I tell you that anyone who looks at a woman lustfully has already committed adultery with her in his heart."
Matthew 5:28

"'Food for the stomach and the stomach for food'—but God will destroy them both. The body is not meant for sexual immorality, but for the Lord, and the Lord for the body. . . . Do you not know that your bodies are members of Christ himself? . . . Flee from sexual immorality. All other sins a man commits are outside his body, but he who sins sexually sins against his own body. Do you not know that your body is a temple of the Holy Spirit, who is in you, whom you have received from God? You are not your own; you were bought at a price. Therefore honor God with your body."
1 Corinthians 6:13, 15, 18-20

Tuesday's Cookies

One of the heartbreaking phenomena of our time has been the abuse of children by their parents. There is no understanding why this should be so, but increasingly child abuse is damaging young psyches, and this damage is seldom repairable over the remainder of their lifetimes. It was after a particularly severe case of such abuse by a man, who sought me out for counsel, that I wrote this metaphor of hope for his child . . . and for all children so damaged by those they trust.

Once there was a very happy little girl who had a very respected mother and father and many wonderful friends. Her father was named Sunday Johnson, her mother was named Monday Johnson, and she was named Tuesday Johnson. They had a cat named August, a dog named Christmas, and a goldfish named Arbor Day. They all rode to church in a red van with "HAPPY" on their designer license plate.

One Wednesday, Monday gave her little Tuesday a beautiful little bag of cookies and left her with her father, Sunday, while she went shopping. They were Tuesday's favorite kind of cookies—chunklate-covered grab crackers. She was so happy, she began to dance excitedly about the room, singing as she danced:

"Chunkalated, chunkalated!
One—two—three!
Grab crackers floating in a chunklate sea!
Roll 'em in the blackberries, dip 'em in your tea!
Chunklate-covered grab crackers all for me!"

It was a song she sang every time she was given her favorite cookies.

While she was singing happily, her father Sunday began to act very strangely. He looked out the windows and smiled on the empty streets. Then he drew all the drapes and shut out the beautiful sunlight. He took Tuesday to a corner of the couch and sat her on his lap. Then he forcefully took the cookies away from her. Tuesday was shocked when Sunday opened her sack of chunklate-covered grab crackers and broke them all in pieces. This made Tuesday feel very ashamed, and so she cried. She always cried when she felt ashamed.

Monday was confused when she came home from her shopping trip and found Tuesday crying.

"What's the matter, dear?" she asked.

"Oh nothing," Tuesday sobbed.

But in a little while, Monday found the bag of broken cookies and gasped. "Tuesday, what happened? Who broke your beautiful cookies?"

Since Tuesday could not bring herself to say, "Daddy!" she simply looked down and said, "I did it!"

When school started in the fall, Tuesday was ashamed to open her sack in front of the other children. So she always sat alone in the lunchroom. She would just sit by herself in the corner of the lunchroom holding her crumpled cookie sack but not opening it. Her teacher, noticing this, approached her and said, "Not hungry, Tuesday?"

The teacher took the crumpled sack and pried Tuesday's fingers away from the folded bag. "Well, no wonder you're not hungry!" said her teacher. "Your cookies are pulverized. Who did this?"

"I did!" lied Tuesday. Then she took some of the crumbles

and started eating them, trying to act as though she preferred pulverized cookies.

And so this same scene began to happen regularly. Many mornings after her mother, Monday, had gone to work, her father would rise, look out the windows. and draw the drapes. Then when all the golden sunlight was gone and the room was very dark, Sunday Johnson would take Tuesday on his lap, and one by one he would crumble her grab crackers, then smile and put them back in her sack, even as tears ran down her face.

But as she got older, she quit crying. She found crying didn't help, and so she worked very hard at loving her father. In fact, after he would break her cookies, she would smile cautiously and say, "Daddy, I love you!" She was convinced that if she said it enough, perhaps one day he would quit drawing the drapes and shutting the sunlight out of her life.

At church her father was a high deacon. Sunday Johnson was loved and respected as a man of God with very high values. All of the church members called him Brother Sunday. It was early in her teenage years that Sunday quit breaking Tuesday's cookies. Still, she was so emotionally scarred that she found it hard to want to be around people. She hated all cookies, and she desperately hated chunklate-covered grab crackers.

When Tuesday was a teenager, she went to a big gospel meeting where she heard her father, Sunday, preaching to a large crowd of more than three hundred young people. He was preaching a very powerful sermon called "Keeping Your Cookies in One Piece!" It was the very first of a whole series on cookies. The next night, Sunday preached another very stern message called "Saving Your Cookies for That One Special Person." His sermon made Tuesday feel so guilty that she quit going to church soon after that.

In her last year of college, Tuesday met another graduating senior whom she felt was just right for her. His name was Friday Jones. He was kind and warm and always considerate. Tuesday began to fall in love with him, and they dated more and more regularly. Only once did he ever bring up the issue of cookies, "Would you like . . ."

But Tuesday threw up her hand like an officer of the law and said, "Please, please! I'm saving my cookies for the right person at the right time!"

Friday laughed. "Me, too! But don't look so severe about it!"

He never asked her to violate her cookie convictions and, in fact, seemed pleased that she had such convictions. But in her heart Tuesday thought to herself, "If only he knew about my father, he would never look at me again."

The days of their courtship flew by and they were married. They had a wonderful wedding, and after the reception when all of the people had gone and they had opened many wonderful presents, they flew away to (wouldn't you know it?) Easter Island for their honeymoon.

They went to their honeymoon cottage.

Friday Jones picked up Tuesday Jones and carried her across the threshold. Then he kicked the door shut and swung her around the room, laughing in the utter joy of their wonderful marriage.

"I love you, Tuesday Johnson!" he shouted out loud in utter pride.

"Not Tuesday Johnson. *Never again* Tuesday Johnson. I'm Tuesday Jones, now!"

They kissed again.

Then as they brightly laughed, Friday pulled out a crisp sack. "Know what I've got here?"

Tuesday blushed but said nothing.

"Chunklate-covered grab crackers!"

Tuesday suddenly began crying. He looked stunned as she pulled out a crumpled sack, full of old and moldy broken cookies. For their entire honeymoon they rarely said a thing. Friday closed his sack of goodies, and Tuesday shyly insisted on putting hers where he would never have to look at her poor crumpled sack again.

Friday was so kind as not to bring up the matter of cookies for the first several months of their lives together. But as soon as they were back from their honeymoon, Tuesday and Friday went to see Dr. Graham Bars, a counselor they had both known for a long time. He was a friend of both their families. While he was surprised to see them, he knew almost immediately why they had come. "Broken cookies?" he asked Tuesday.

"Yes," she said looking down.

"Wait here, you two." Dr. Bars said. "He got up and abruptly left the room. In moment he came back with a huge tube that had the words COOKIE GLUE lettered on the side.

So Tuesday and Friday Jones and Dr. Graham Bars worked for seven months on the way to put broken cookies back together again.

Just when they were beginning to despair that Tuesday's cookies would ever be mended, Tuesday had an experience that was totally unexpected. It happened right after Friday went to work one morning. Tuesday was by herself in their little apartment having a cup of coffee when she walked to the window and looked out into the sunny street. There was a tall man, standing on the sidewalk just in front of her home. It was a Baker, dressed all in white. And though he said nothing, he reached out his hands toward her with a brand new sack. She thought she knew what was in the sack, but she was afraid of all men with sacks. She became so agitated, she dropped her coffee cup. Tears flooded her eyes. She reached for the draw cord and closed the drapes.

Now she was terribly unnerved! She had the feeling that while she had shut the Baker out in the street, he was now in the very room with her. Then a voice broke in the darkened room around her: "It does little good to try and glue your cookies while your soul is splintered. The guilt you bear was never yours. Love first the Baker, and the cookies are forever there!"

"But I am soiled . . . despised . . . broken . . ."

"Those are my words to bear, not yours. Your words are clean, loved, and whole."

"Then give me these words for my own, and I will be healed!"

She whirled around the room, as delirious as when she was a child. In a pirouette of joy, she grabbed the draw cord of the drapes and swished the curtains wide open. Sunlight flew into the room, like a tidal wave of newness.

And then she saw it, sitting on the table, awfully close to the Bible she had carried in her wedding. It was there! A sack! A crisp, new sack! And on the side it said simply, "Bon Appetit! The Baker!" Tremblingly she opened the bag. She knew it. There they were: chunklate-covered grab crackers! Tears flowed freely down her cheeks and she knew she was whole.

When Friday walked up to the door of his apartment that evening, he noticed that Tuesday had already set the trash out for the collectors the next morning. There in the top of the container he saw the half-used tube of "Cookie Glue."

"Good!" he thought to himself, "That stuff wasn't working anyway!"

He was about to open the door and walk in, when he heard Tuesday singing from inside a little song he had never heard her sing before. It was an odd song, a familiar and yet not so familiar old cookie rhyme:

"Chunkalated, chunkalated!
One—Two—Three . . ."

He wondered only for a moment, and then Friday smiled even as he opened the door. There stood Tuesday holding out towards him a brand new sack of cookies. He took her in his arms. He was delighted.

With the passing of time, all of their neighbors knew there was no happier couple in the world. And often, when Friday and Tuesday were together cooking out or enjoying the last warm days of summer, they could be heard singing that old nursery rhyme of children whose lives are happily untarnished by shadows.

"Chunkalated, chunkalated!
One—Two—Three!
Grab crackers floating in a chunklate sea!
Roll 'em in blackberries, dip 'em in your tea!
Chunkalated grab crackers all for me!"

Foolish men who accuse a woman mindlessly—you cannot even see you cause what you abuse."
Juana Inés de la Cruz, *Hombres Necios* (Foolish Men)

"It would be better for him to be thrown into the sea with a millstone tied around his neck than for him to cause one of these little ones to sin."
Luke 17:2

"Fathers, do not exasperate your children; instead, bring them up in the training and instruction of the Lord."
Ephesians 6:4

Poor Little Jack

One psychologist, whose lore I honor, says that we men think about sex seventy-five percent of our waking time. I like thinking I do better than the more lusty. Nevertheless, given this universal masculine affliction, parents ought to be somewhat tolerant. Little Jack Horner was no doubt cornered by a lot of appetites. He makes me wish mothers could be more understanding.

Little Jack Horner sat in the corner,
Clouded and thoroughly vexed,
Full well he knew he had broken taboo,
And questioned his mother on sex.

"Jack," she screamed, "Lad, you are filthy and bad
To ask such a question as that!
The thoughts you employ are X-rated, boy,
Your father will give you a spat."

So Jack had to find he had a foul mind
For asking his question on sex,
And so there began to develop a man
With a devious kind of complex.

Confused now and then, Jack never again
Would question his mother and dad.
The reprimand stern had helped him to learn,
That sex was all ugly and bad.

Confident, sure, he grew more mature,
But the sex-ban had its affect.
It became very true, Jack always withdrew
From all future mention of sex.

Years had gone by, when in dickey and tie,
Jack stood at the altar with pride.
The reception was nice, and pelted with rice,
He eagerly kissed his new bride.

Something went wrong—it didn't last long—
Though no one ever knew why.
And no one suspects the awful complex
That caused a young marriage to die.

But the issues are steep, and the roots go quite deep
To the time when Jack was a lad.
When nobody other than his very own mother
Had made him feel sex was all bad.

"The Way of Heaven is to benefit others and not to injure."
Lao-tzu, *The Way of Lao-tzu*

"You might as well fall flat on your face as lean over too far backward."
James Thurber, *The Bear Who Let It Alone*

"No one, sir," she said. "Then neither do I condemn you," Jesus declared.
"Go now and leave your life of sin."
John 8:11

"Train up a child in the way he should go: and when he is old he will not
depart from it."
Proverbs 22:6 (KJV)

"Marriage is honorable in all, and the bed undefiled."
Hebrews 13:4 (KJV)

"A double minded man is unstable in all his ways."
James 1:8 (KJV)

Ralph

This piece is fictional but frighteningly honest. Maybe a dab of fiction is the way to make every man's near-biography honest . . . and edgy.

I met Ralph in the smoking section of the bar in the Monteleone Hotel in New Orleans. It was late on Friday night, April 3, 1987. I was waiting for a single table in the main restaurant and was stirring a pinch of lime into a tumbler of tomato juice when I caught sight of him. The light was so dim that it seemed on the verge of going out completely in that section of the restaurant.

My eyes first fell on Ralph when I became aware that something in the shadows had cleared its throat. The hair rose on the nape of my neck. My vision fingered the darkness to see what was invisibly there. I stared hard at the dim emptiness and tentatively asked, "Is someone there?"

"I am," said Ralph.

The voice issued from nowhere. I slitted my eyes now to laser-focus, straining to poke holes in the darkness, working hard to make any two molecules of substance gather themselves in the aching absence. I pushed back my chair and stood to move to a section of the bar that was better lit.

"Move if you will," it said, "but your movement will not keep me from stalking you."

I sat back down and stared hard through the semi-darkness. Then I saw it was the intruder, a thin, milk-white hologram of a soul, so thinly visible that I could see a wall-plug through its transparent body. I shuddered. The thing had a face.

"Yes, I have a face," he said, "Does it look familiar?"

I trembled.

The thing had my face!

It was then that I realized it even talked like me!

"What's your name, Banquo?" I asked.

"Very funny," said the shadowy thing. "My name is Raphael, but you can call me Ralph. I'm your guardian angel."

"Excuse me, but I'm fifty years old. Why have you waited till now to show up?"

"I've been around since you've been around. For five decades now I've never been more than a few feet from you. If you are just now seeing me, it's because you have never experienced .532 degree half-light. When that precise level of illumination occurs, guardians become visible, or mostly so.

"You see, my good doctor, you mortals rarely experience this precise level of illumination, and only at this level can my realm visibly touch your realm. So gaze at me and see what may be seen. It will likely never happen again in your life. Still, for the rest of your life I will be here."

"But, I hear you as well as see you. What has illumination to do with that?"

"At such moments as angels are visible, they're also audible."

"I am surprised," I said, "that we look so much alike!"

"Believe me, our look-alike status is no more distasteful to you than it is to us." Ralph paused and then went on, "I've come to tell you a story. All angels are troubled about our human similarity. Nothing personal, but balding and cellulite are not considered beautiful in *either* of our realms, I'm afraid."

I moved back into the shadows and listened as Ralph continued.

"There was once a boy born shortly after the Great Depression had begun to recede. He was born in a large family whose poverty might have been eased, if the boy's father had not been such a terrible drunkard. Finally, just before the outbreak of World War II, his father's drinking habit had become so severe that he was often thrown in jail for public misdemeanors and unruly drunkenness. Once when his father was jailed, the boy's mother obtained a legal separation and the father abandoned the boy's family.

"Without his father the small boy was often disconsolate and felt very afraid. During World War II the boy's older siblings entered the service as the wives of American servicemen. This further increased the boy's feelings of loneliness. Often as a child his insecurities haunted him with bad dreams and engulfing depression. Then in 1945 the war was over, and the boy became a believer in Christ."

"Ralph," I interrupted, "this story has a familiar ring about it."

"It's a story you may know well, but it is not your story." He was most insistent, so I grew quiet and let him continue.

"Well, this childhood commitment that had led him to know Christ was but the beginning of a long love affair. For reasons the boy could not explain, he was possessed of a desperate hunger to know Christ better and better. He was mad with joy. He sang the Sunday School songs and memorized Scriptures. He prayed, as children pray, with all his heart. It never occurred to the child that there were more things to believe in than he believed. He thought there were no other ways to see the world than he saw it. He looked at the world only briefly, side glanced, and then returned his young eyes toward Jesus.

"Here and there the harsher world came into view. Once he was beaten up by a group of sidewalk ruffians, who seemed to have no motive for their assault except that they enjoyed the sport of their own hoodlumery. The boy cried all the way home, and when he reached home his mother consoled him. It was strange that he really didn't seem to need her consolation. The trials of his childhood were not especially easy for him, but they did engender a furious need for God, and with each of them he seemed to develop a growing spiritual closeness.

"His adolescence was in some ways typical. He found himself walled in by growing feelings of a maturing sexuality. Sometimes the rise of these new feelings obliterated his best resolve, and his mental permissiveness caused him to wonder if he would ever be free enough of his fantasies to be of much use to God. But for the most part he studied his books and found himself reasonably reasonable about most things."

"Stop, Ralph!" I was almost shouting. "I tell you this story is mine! I know its outcome, and quite frankly I'm bored!"

"Don't flatter yourself. The story is not yours. You never have been this story. Believe me, the story will all too soon be dissimilar from yours. Now . . . lets see, I was about to say that in his sixteenth year, the boy had a terrible nightmare. His quiet life was invaded one midnight by a demon named Gloria."

"A girl demon?" I was relieved. This was the first time in the relating of his narrative that the story did not seem to be my own.

"Yes! A girl demon, or so it appeared—although the whole supernatural realm of demons and angels is essentially sexless. But demons may for deviant purposes appear any way they like, and while Gloria's name was probably something

Screwtapish, like Scabheart, as far as the boy could see, she was a woman.

"She was plenty seductive, too! Not in any sexual sort of a way, but in a way that seemed to say, 'Come hither, son, and I will make you wise.'

"'Get thee behind me, Satan!' said the boy. So ordered, she left the room—but only for a few days. Several nights later she returned after the boy had gone to sleep. He woke in the wee small hours of the morning to find her simply sitting in the corner of his room, smiling, waiting, and oddly beckoning to him with her finger crooked. Sometimes she slouched enticingly in a chair and used her seductive, glistening body to lure the boy toward a kind of carnality that tempted him with such fantasies that it became increasingly harder for him to say, 'Get thee behind me, Satan!' She drew upon his blossoming, adolescent sexuality far more seductively than any of the sirens that vexed Ulysses and his men."

"So Gloria was one of those late puberty demons?" I interjected. "Ralph, this boy you speak of is no different than any other boy. Which of us on waking up in puberty have not known Gloria? She is cheerleader, tight jeans, *femme fantasia*. She is that seductress of emerging masculinity, all staple-in-the-navel centerfold. All men have known Gloria, Ralph."

Ralph ignored my interruption, pressing ahead with his tale. "Gloria always came to the boy with a condemning grin on her face as though she knew, sooner or later, she would win over his reluctance. He never spoke to her, though she came and went in his room for over a year. Then one day he never saw her again."

"Not possible, Ralph!" I said. "Gloria is there all our lives. Trust me on this one. None of you sexless angels and demons can possibly understand this one. Better leave it alone. Gloria haunts the male psyche for as long as a man lives. Who do you think poses for those porno pictorials? It's Gloria. So if you're trying to tell me that one day Gloria just walked out of the boy's life, I'm sorry. I'm just not buying your story.

"There was a seventy-nine year old man I knew who used to lecture on marital fidelity. At the conclusion of his lecture, one of the young married men in the class asked him, 'Sir, about what age do men quit looking at pretty girls?' The old man wryly answered, 'Well, sonny, I don't know for sure, but I do know its sometime after seventy-nine!'

"So you see, Ralph, Gloria never quits hanging around the red-blooded men of this world. She runs the counters of every adult bookstore in this nation. She does the can-can at every 'Red Mill' in France, too."

I was talking pretty straight with Ralph. But I knew that he simply didn't understand Gloria.

"If you're ever invited to lecture on the male mystique, Ralph, turn it down."

Again Ralph ignored my dialogue . . . and continued.

"The boy graduated from high school at seventeen. He determined that he would devote himself to the Boss. He loved God. He was singular about this. He couldn't stand the long intervals between Sundays, for he did so love to worship. Any thought that came from his mind which was not about Jesus was a thought wasted. He determined that he would become a foreign missionary, and thus he started off to college.

"He was a natural student in many ways and his grades were excellent. As a missionary in the making, he was determined to teach rather than preach. He was not trying to be overly humble in selecting a teaching career over a pulpit ministry. He just never felt as though he was capable of so high a calling.

"It was during his sophomore year in college that two very different events were to impact his life. First, the Russians put up the first space satellite. This event caused an outcry that America was lagging behind the rest of the world in the teaching of the sciences. Since the boy was majoring in . . ."

"Excuse me, did this boy have a name?" I interrupted.

"How about Clay?"

"Fine, Clay."

"Well, Clay was now assured that he was on the right track. He was majoring in science in a world that needed scientists. He knew that God wanted him to teach science on some foreign mission field. So now he was settled. He studied hard to be worthy of what he believed was the highest calling of all. He would teach those who had never had a chance at education, helping them come to treasure education.

"Further, never did a day go by that he did not enter into prayer, so that his own devotional life would not just see him teach science but that he would live in a growing bond with Christ. He hungered to belong to Christ. At moments when there was a lull in his studies, he would worship Christ. He was a living, walking, breathing testament of grace. He practiced the presence of God. His soul longed for God as the deer longs after the waterbrook. He would walk alone in the darkness and meditate upon the glory of Christ and the riches of their relationship. He even applied to go on to seminary once his college days were ended.

"He had begun to look forward to this time of new spiritual growth in his life. In seminary he would deepen his faith and ready himself to begin his service abroad. But as much as he desired that glorious time of future study, he never hurried a moment. He believed that the only place one can meet Christ is in the moment. He rose in the morning to praise Christ, and Jesus was the last word on his tongue when he closed his eyes in sleep each night.

"This dream would have gone on forever, except that at the beginning of his junior year in college, Gloria came back."

"The demon?" Ralph looked annoyed at my interruption.

"Yes," he went on, "the demon. Only now she wasn't a demon any longer. Now she was a real, live person."

"Aha! Now we're getting down to it," I cried. "I told you, Ralph, they never go away!" I had gotten so loud in my rebuke of Ralph that two men looking at a street map of New Orleans both turned and looked across the bar in my direction. I made a note to let Ralph go on talking. He was quieter than I was. The two men looked back at the map, and Ralph began again.

"Gloria took an immediate fancy to Clay. She grinned like the demon that had haunted his adolescence. Whenever she did this, it unnerved Clay, for he could not help but remember how fearful those early days had been. She was a beautiful girl and so alluring that merely walking her across campus on a moonlit evening would stir his libido to a near frenzy. Twice she invited him up to her room for drinks and the 'chance to get to know her better.' Twice he refused, but it was much harder the second time.

"Gloria was also rich, as was her father. She promised him that if things continued to work between them, she could guarantee him that her father would give him a six-figure job and his own Corvette. She would often lure him from his studies on a beautiful afternoon. If Clay was utterly devoted to his studies, she would remind him that it was not 'what you know but *who* you know in life that causes you to win or lose.' Finally she talked Clay into leaving church on Sundays here and there so they could go to the lake or to one of the shopping malls of the city.

"One beautiful Sunday, Gloria picked up Clay and they went for a drive. They had a late, leisurely dinner, then continued driving far into the late afternoon. Gloria had stuck a card in the pocket of her blouse. It was a plain white card, but she had blotted her lipstick on it and then folded it around a condom. She had told her roommate that her intention was to 'wean Clay from his Victorian lifestyle.' Clay, of course, had no knowledge of her intentions and, incapable of suspicion, he went with Gloria to spend the day, captured by both her beauty and the overwhelming spell of a late summer afternoon.

"Their drive lasted a long time. Gloria always allowed Clay to do the driving, even though the car was hers. Both of them realized that the kind of car she could afford was beyond the resources of a budding missionary.

At length Clay pulled the car to a stop and parked her Mercedes SL on a lonely country road, and they both walked back from the road to a waterfall. Several times along the way, they stopped and Clay drew Gloria up to him and kissed her. The daylight had now spent itself, wasting its golden sunlight on yellow fields and on a thousand darkening landscapes.

"Evening began coming on, and as they moved further through the woods towards the roaring cascade, Clay felt a surge of passion such as he had never felt before. At the beautiful pool, Gloria unbuttoned his shirt. He reciprocated by unbuttoning her blouse. He suddenly was so overcome with passion that he crushed her against himself and smothered her with kisses.

"As he held her against himself, he suddenly felt something sticking him sharply in his chest. He pushed Gloria reluctantly away and noticed a piece of paper in the pocket of her blouse. It was more like a card than a piece of paper, and he pulled it out of her pocket. He unfolded the card at its sharp crease. The light was very dim in the heavy foliage by the waterfall. In fact, it was exactly .532 degree half-light."

"Don't tell me! Clay's guardian showed up and saved his chastity!" I wished I hadn't interrupted Ralph.

"Clay's guardian did, in fact, show up. And as Clay held the card in his hand, the guardian said, 'Take and read.'

"Listen, Ralph, I've read Augustine. Let me guess: the card read, 'Let us walk honestly, as in the day; not in rioting and drunkenness, not in chambering and wantonness, not in strife and envying. But put ye on the Lord Jesus Christ, and make not provision for the flesh, to fulfill the lusts thereof (Romans 13:13-14).' But if there was nothing written on the card, where did those words from Romans come from? How did the Scripture get on the card?"

"Some wonderful things happen in .532 degree half-light, son. You see, Augustine was right about irresistible grace. Sometimes the Boss saves people from themselves. Sodom and Gomorrah prove that we should never count on it, but Rahab proves that once in a while the Boss acts to spare us even when we are precipitously near to consenting to evil. Who can understand the Boss? His ways are inscrutable.

"Well, no sooner was the Scripture out of his mouth than Gloria fell to the ground. There was now laughter all around Clay in this primeval glen—laughter so shrill that it nearly blunted the lovely roar of the waterfall. Gloria was suddenly gone.

"Clay reached down to pick up her blouse, which had fallen to the ground when she disappeared. When he lifted it up, he uncovered the writhing form of a snake. It didn't frighten him. He knew enough about snakes to know it wasn't poisonous. He thought of crushing it beneath his heel . . . "

"There's a verse of scripture like that in Genesis," I said.

"But," Ralph went on, "it was somehow too connected with Gloria for him to step on. 'No,' mused Clay, 'I can't step on you. I just took you to dinner . . . I almost . . .'

"Clay realized that it was his 'almost' that had almost destroyed him. He was alone now with his guardian, who said to him, 'Come on, Clay. The .532 degree half-light won't hold much longer. I've got to get you out of these woods before it gets too dark for you to see me—and before it's too dark for you to find your way out.'

"Even as he began to follow the guardian out of the woods, Clay could see that Gloria's clothes were being absorbed into the earth, and soon all traces of her would be gone. The snake watched him leave, but even before Clay left, he broke a chunk of bark off the tree where Gloria had so recently melted away."

"Why?" I asked.

"The guardian said that as Clay walked away from the waterfall, he kept fingering the roughness of the tree bark in his hand and incessantly repeating, 'But of the fruit of the tree that is in the midst of the garden, God hath said, ye shall not eat of it, neither shall ye touch it, lest ye die' (Genesis 3:3)."

"Clay is an old man now. Sometimes he will look wistfully into the distant horizons and say oddly to himself, 'of every tree but one . . .' Then he seems to see a better tree, and he repeats in low tones, 'And he showed to me a pure river of the water of life, clear as crystal, proceeding out of the throne of God and of the Lamb . . . and on either side of the river, there was a tree of life' (Revelation 22:1-2)."

"But what of the Mercedes SL?" I asked.

"Vanished!" said Ralph.

"So the coach at last turns back to a pumpkin, and Clay's purity paves his way to the foreign mission field? What is this: a kind of fairy tale for Christians? A marriage of the Cinderella story to missions and demonology?"

Again ignoring me, Ralph plodded on: "Clay walked back to town that night along dark and lonely roads. He knew what Gloria was. She was not merely a temptress; she was a constant bid for an alternative to reality. She could have been Clay's any night he called. She was appetite gratification. She was wealth. She was image and self-esteem.

"He knew, too, that most missionaries and pastors knew Gloria. They kept her in a room at the back of their minds. They had all been to the same tree. They had all been reminded by guardians huddling in half-light that Romans 13:13 was to be reckoned with. But most of them went on keeping Gloria around. They permitted themselves a quasi-commitment they could talk about but they didn't have to take too seriously. They made commitments to Christ in public covenants, but they permitted themselves the same little books and pictures they used to see passed under desks in geometry class. They drove hot cars and made six-digit salaries, while they promised publicly to die for Christ in poverty and submission.

"But as I said, Clay is an old man. He works in a village of thatched huts in one of the islands of Polynesia. He walks among the islanders teaching them of the very Christ he never seems to get enough of. He is up each morning just before the sun rises. And on three separate occasions in that split second of time, he has experienced .532 degree half-light. He likes looking at his guardian every now and then, just to remind himself that our world is not the only world there is.

"On a crude, carved shelf in his home, there are two odd artifacts that create the only altar of remembrance he permits himself: a piece of bark he broke from a tree near a waterfall, and a creased card. The card has nothing written on it most of the time, but at those few special moments of .532 degree half-light, a couple of verses from Romans are clearly written there.

"Clay is the wealthiest man I know. He is rich with a love affair that so possesses him, he is ashamed that he nearly lost it all at an old tree. One of these days, I suspect that Clay and Christ will be walking along in the constant conversation that absorbs his days, and he will be permitted to pass through the gates to find his redemption—the glorious end of his life."

By now, I was weeping. "Ralph, you are right! This is not my story."

"I know it is not your story. You have no chunk of bark on your low-altar shelf."

I thought of Jesus, and how I once had loved him. "No, this is not my story," I repeated, weeping even harder.

"Ah, but it might have been . . . it might have been," he said.

Suddenly a woman with a camera stepped toward us. She was one of those photographers who take pictures of people in hotel restaurants and bring them to your table just before you're finishing your dessert.

"NO, DON'T DO IT!" I shouted at her, just as the flash

went off. But it was too late. The .532 degree half-light was eradicated by an explosion of blue-white incandescence. Ralph was gone. I have not seen him since.

When the searing light had died and my eyes had adjusted, I found the woman with the camera. "Please, madam, while I won't be staying for dinner, I would like a copy of that picture you took."

"To be sure, sir. I'll have it in fifteen minutes at the cashier's stand."

We met again in fifteen minutes. "You're not going to like this picture, sir," she apologized. "I didn't realize you were crying when I took it." I slipped the photo from its envelope and studied it a moment. It was true. I was obviously crying in the picture. My face was streaked with grief.

"It's perfect! How much is it?" I asked her.

"Fifteen dollars, but . . . sir, you don't have to take this one. I can snap another of you and have it ready in half an hour." It was then that I looked down and saw her Monteleone Hotel nametag. It read, "Gloria."

"I should have known." I said.

"Pardon me, sir. Have we ever met?"

"You'll never know how often."

I could see that she was puzzled as I walked out of the hotel into the streets.

As I said before, this happened back in 1987. Further, I have now put up a small shelf in my home. There's nothing on that shelf except a photograph of a none-too-saintly old sinner, caught in the act of crying.

I also keep a plain white card near the picture. I feel sure that at regular intervals of day and night when the light measures

.532 degree half-light, some pretty important words come and go on that unmarked card.

For the most part, I delight in knowing I need never deny myself the fullness of God's pleasure. I am content in Christ. Still, I always wonder what I might have been.

"I've looked on a lot of women with lust. I've committed adultery in my heart many times. This is something that God recognized I will do—and I have done it—and God forgives me for it."
Jimmy Carter, interview in *Playboy* magazine

"You are doing the things your own father does."
John 8:41

"Do not be anxious about anything, but in everything, by prayer and petition, with thanksgiving, present your requests to God. And the peace, which transcends all understanding, will guard your hearts and your minds in Christ Jesus. Finally, brothers, whatever is true, whatever is noble, whatever is right, whatever is pure, whatever is lovely, whatever is admirable—if anything is excellent or praiseworthy—think about such things."
Philippians 4:6-8

The Lawn Mower Man
and the Church Lady

Faith Hits Home

The Lawn Mower Man and the Church Lady

Synthesis is always the best solution to a quarrel . . . maybe even a religious quarrel.

Once upon a time, there was a hairy galoot named Victor, who married a thin little slip of a freckled woman named Gladys. Victor irritated Gladys, because on Sunday, Victor mowed the lawn while Gladys went to church.

"Why don't you go to church with me, Victor?" said Gladys each Sunday as she left the house. She said these weekly words to Victor's rump as he bent over his mower, pouring gas from a little red can.

Their lifestyles became very separate because Gladys always went to church and never helped Victor mow the lawn. Victor dumped clippings while Gladys read her quarterly.

"What if your mower explodes some Sunday?" said Gladys one night while Victor was sharpening a mower blade. "Well, what if your church falls in during a sermon?" said Victor.

They didn't talk to each other much as they grew older. Once in a while Gladys would sourly say, "What if it explodes?" Victor would only sneer and say, "What if it caves in?"

Finally, Gladys became so mad about Victor always mowing the lawn, she quit speaking to him. Victor became so mad about Gladys always going to church and never helping him with the lawn mowing, he wouldn't speak to her either. After this period of silence had gone on for some time, Victor taped a note to Gladys's dressing mirror. The paper only contained two lines:

"I wish just once you'd help me with the lawn. And I hope it caves in."

Gladys was pretty mad, too. So she taped a two-line note to Victor's mirror:

"I wish just once you'd go to church with me. And I hope it explodes."

Two Sundays later, soon after Gladys left for church, Victor's lawn mower just caved in like a soft orange. Since he couldn't mow the lawn anyway, he quickly showered and started off for church, thinking maybe he would go to church just once.

About the same time as he left for church, there was a loud furnace explosion in the church, and Gladys ran out coughing because of the furnace fumes. Since she couldn't stay for church anyway, she said, "I think I'll go home and help Victor mow the lawn." They met on the sidewalk halfway between their home and the church.

"Oh, Victor, the church exploded!"

"Oh, Gladys, the lawn mower caved in!"

They embraced.

"Thank God, you're safe," said Victor.

"Let's hire a lawn mowing service," said Gladys.

Victor joined the church six weeks later, and Gladys was very happy. They sang hymns, although Victor had a rather croaky voice. And they read Scriptures, although Gladys had to hold the Bible nearly to her knees because her bifocals needed changing.

"I just love going to church," said Victor.

Gladys beamed. "I'll tell you what. Why don't we do something to help our little church? Why don't we mow the church lawn together . . . that is, if the mower doesn't explode."

He kissed her sweetly, in a churchy way. Naturally, Gladys caved in.

Marriage, *n*. A community consisting of a master, a mistress, and two slaves, making in all, two."
Ambrose Bierce, *The Devil's Dictionary*

"For this reason a man will leave his father and mother and be united to his wife, and the two will become one flesh."
Matthew 19:5

"Submit to one another out of reverence for Christ. Wives, submit to your husbands as to the Lord. For the husband is the head of the wife as Christ is the head of the church, his body, of which he is the Savior. Now as the church submits to Christ, so also wives should submit to their husbands in everything. Husbands, love your wives, just as Christ loved the church and gave himself up for her."
Ephesians 5:21-25

If You Would Just . . .

We live in misery when we cannot master the same art of unconditional acceptance which God ever extends to us. "Just As I Am" is a great hymn to sing to God. "Just As You Are" is a great hymn to sing to others.

Ethel had always had a long, long nose. In grade school the kids all called her "Beaky" until she ran into the restroom and cried. She was nearly thirty before Elmer asked to marry her. (Elmer had a fairly long nose himself.) She said, "Yes, of course, I'll marry you, but what about my nose?"

"What nose?" asked Elmer.

This was clearly the man for her.

So she married Elmer, who loved her and never seemed to notice the length of her nose.

But Ethel was not so gracious. Though her own nose had been fully accepted, she felt Elmer's nose was just too long, and she didn't mind saying so.

"It's too long, Elmer!" said Ethel, looking straight at Elmer's nose. "If you would just have it clipped, you'd be a good-looking man."

Elmer felt bad, but he trusted Ethel. Every time she said, "Elmer, if you would just . . ." she would tell him something that was good for him. Now she was telling him the plain truth. His nose was too long.

He remembered their marriage. He'd finally agreed to it after she'd said, "Elmer, if you would just say 'I do,' we both would find a real life together filled with happiness forever." So Elmer said, "I do."

Ethel was half right. Elmer was happy, but Ethel was ill at ease with Elmer. After all, there were so many things wrong with him.

One of the first things Ethel had said to him on their honeymoon was that he snored so loud she couldn't sleep. "If you would just have your adenoids out, I could be truly happy with you." So Elmer went to an E.N.T. surgeon and had his adenoids out. He quit snoring, but Ethel wasn't entirely happy.

When Elmer saw her looking at his neck mole, he could have said it before she did. "Elmer, if you would just have that mole taken off your neck . . ." It wasn't much of a trick. It cost sixty-five dollars in outpatient charges. Presto! No more neck mole!

The overlap incisors were the same. "Elmer, if you would just . . ."

"Oh, Ethel, of course," said Elmer, not letting her finish. An oral surgeon finished the task, and Ethel was happy for a week or so. But soon Ethel pointed out that his tonsils were always infected and probably responsible for his halitosis. "Elmer, if you would just . . ." So, of course, he did.

He was in the basement meditating on who he should call about the nose clip when Ethel made her way down the rickety steps and found him sitting in a dark corner. When her eyes fully adjusted, she saw a crude shelf with a sign over it. The sign said, "ELMER, IF YOU WOULD JUST . . ." On the shelf was a series of bottles labeled with dates and filled with clear solutions. Inside each of the bottles were things like moles and teeth and adenoids and tonsils. On the last bottle was written "Nose Tip," all ready to be dated when his surgery was over.

"Ethel . . ." Elmer hesitated, "I was about to call a plastic surgeon."

"Why, Elmer, if you would just . . ."

She stopped and looked at the sign over the shelf. Suddenly she felt ashamed. She realized what a terrible game this "if you would just" business was.

"Elmer," she went on, "I want you to postpone that nose clip. I want to get mine clipped first."

"But darling, I like your nose the way it is!"

"Elmer, are you sure?"

He stood up and kissed her sweetly on the tip of her long proboscis. "Ethel, I know how to make our marriage perfect."

"I do, too, Elmer, but go ahead and say it."

"If you would just quit saying, 'If you would just . . .'"

"Marriages are made in heaven and consummated on earth."
John Lyly, *Mother Bombie*

"So in everything, do to others what you would have them do to you, for this sums up the Law and the Prophets."
Matthew 7:12

"Wives, in the same way be submissive to your husbands so that, if any of them do not believe the word, they may be won over without words by the behavior of their wives."
1 Peter 3:1

Little Boy, Where Are You?

In the spirit of a James Kavanaugh poem of the same title, I wrote this poem for the Green Bay Packers. I got to pray with the Packers on Thanksgiving Day, 1994, just before their game with Dallas. I remain convinced that public opinion spoils the innocence each of us needs to be winners.

Little boy, where are you?

I've been looking everywhere for you.
I gotta play a big game today
    and I want to play football
    like you used to play it.

I need you back!

What I really liked about you, little boy,
    was that you got excited about the right things,
Like flexing that little lump of a bicep
    and asking your Dad to feel it.
Like sawing back and forth over the center bar of your bike,
    and wobbling your way to the market
    with your pant leg rolled up
    so you wouldn't get your jeans caught in the chain.
Back then you cried about the right things,
    like when your puppy got run over,
    not after you read the sports page after a dumb play.
And you didn't limit your French fries,
    'cause grease and salt tasted good together.

And you didn't worry
    about what people you didn't like said about you
    'cause it was real stupid to try to please the people
    you didn't like.
You kept your goals simple, too,
    because you knew that the things you needed
    to make you really happy were pretty simple.
Like finding that first black hair
    that told you you'd someday be like your daddy.
Or when the corner grocer gave you a king-sized Baby Ruth
    because you played so well.
Or when your junior high coach welcomed you into manhood
    by using that not-too-bad cuss word that said,
    "We men gotta use them kind of words
    so we won't sound too much like girls."

I need you back, little boy.
I've been looking everywhere for you,
    'cause I can still remember
    your thin little arm in your oversized sleeve,
    throwing that ball 'cause you wanted to win.
You threw good back then,
    even if your pass wobbled a little bit,
    and you couldn't get it far enough down the field.
Still it was a good pass,
    and good was how you felt when you threw it,
    and good was how you dreamed.
Back then you played football because you loved it,
    not because you signed a contract to do it.
You played real good
    'cause your mind was clean, and your heart,

and nobody had junked it up by selling you some
bogus national image
or television angles or instant replays.

I tell you, I need you back, little boy,
because I've gotten too concerned about how I look
or whether or not I'll get off the bench
or how I'll explain myself to the board
or whether or not I'll get invited to the press conference.
I've forgotten how to do my own driving.
I've forgotten the simplicity of being my own man.

Where are you, little boy?
It's Thanksgiving.
I gotta play a big game.
I've been looking everywhere for you.

"As long as you know that most men are like children,
you know everything."
Coco Chanel

"Age does not make us children, as they say.
It only finds us true children still."
Johann Wolfgang von Goethe, *Faust*

"When the chief priests and the teachers of the law saw the wonderful
things he did and the children shouting in the temple area, 'Hosanna to
the Son of David,' they were indignant. 'Do you hear what these children
are saying?' they asked him. 'Yes,' replied Jesus, 'have you never read,
"From the lips of children and infants you have ordained praise?"'"
Matthew 21:15-16

"Therefore, since we are surrounded by such a great cloud of witnesses,
let us throw off everything that hinders and the sin that so easily entangles,
and let us run with perseverance the race marked out for us. Let us fix our
eyes on Jesus, the author and perfecter of our faith, who for the joy set
before him endured the cross, scorning its shame, and sat down at the
right hand of the throne of God."
Hebrews 12:1-2

"Then said I, Ah, Lord GOD! behold, I cannot speak: for I am a child. But
the LORD said unto me, Say not, I am a child; for thou shalt go to all that I
shall send thee, and whatsoever I shall command thee thou shalt speak."
Jeremiah 1:6-7 (KJV)

"For as many as are led by the Spirit of God, they are the sons of God.
For ye have not received the spirit of bondage again to fear; but ye have
received the Spirit of adoption, whereby we cry, Abba, Father. The Spirit
itself beareth witness with our spirit, that we are the children of God."
Romans 8:14-16 (KJV)

The Diet

It's so hard for me not to try and get God and the devil involved in my overweight-and-binge-diet lifestyle. Heaven must be the place for glorified bodies, and hell the last resort of those who find themselves powerless before a pan of brownies.

I'm thirty-five sit-ups behind for the week,
I'm killing myself by degrees
By trying to jog for a mile and a half
On Rye Crisp and dry cottage cheese.

But the chocolate I ate on Valentine's Day
And the homemade ice cream in July
And the turkey and eggnog I should have dismissed
Have joined with the ugly mince pie.

And now I atone in sweatshirt and pants
(My attitude, squarely, is blah)
I pedal my old cycle-ciser a mile
With the tension set on "Ooh-lah-lah."

Of leg drops, I've done a full twenty-five
(On the twentieth I wanted to die)
And then when it's time for my celery stick break,
I drink diet cola and cry.

If we could but look for a moment or two
On all that heaven must be,
We'd find it eternally brownies and cream,
Delicious, but calorie-free.

And hell would be a vast, ghastly land
With worn old bathroom scales.
Where chubbies weighed every five minutes
And jogged and ate lettuce and wailed.

"Tell me what you eat, and I shall tell you what you are."
Anthelme Brillat-Savarin, *La Physiologie du Goût* (The Physiology of Taste)

"Therefore I tell you, do not worry about your life, what you will eat; or
about your body, what you will wear."
Luke 12:22

"So whether you eat or drink or whatever you do,
do it all for the glory of God."
1 Corinthians 10:31

Two

I have two old friends who, after forty years of marriage to other mates, learned to spell "hope" in the simple syllable of a second chance.

I wondered how each had found the other.

They were two whose togetherness with other loves
    had shared other children, other laughter,
    other pain in separate worlds.
Each had watched their first beloved
    strangled in the tentacles of melanoma.
Each had buried hope in gagging
    grief and blaring silence.

Each had walked that long, long way
    from hearse to grave and back again.
Each had stared into the dark of empty bedrooms
    and felt the hot tears slash an older, wiser face.
Each had learned to set the table for one—
    that staring-straight-ahead obscenity—
    one plate, one fork, one crystal glass
    that didn't mind a thumbprint
    when there was no one there to see it.

They remembered how they both felt the cold
    seep up from the chilled, unheated earth
    around the new sod graves of their first loves.
Brutality was now the cruel instruction of their choice.

Years ago they had picked other mates.
They chose as young lovers always choose—
    mates to flatter all their self-importance when others said,
    "Isn't he handsome?"
    "Isn't she beautiful?"
    "And wasn't he a catch, with his degrees and income?"
    "And isn't she just right?
        Her father was the mayor, you know!"
And so they dated most conspicuously.
Their engagement photograph in all the papers,
    making all who knew them near-neurotics
    lest their wedding gifts prove not quite right
    for such a just right pair.

Flattered by their youth,
    these separate lovers picked their first low-mortgage house.
It was not the house they hoped to own
    when they would later keep up with the Joneses.
It was just a house that they could occupy until they saved the
    money that would buy their noble dream.
But age makes older lovers wise,
    and from the back side of the hearse,
    each lost a love and found the truth.
They were captive in those younger years
    to all the world wanted them to be:
    and they were perfect, and felt perfect
    before life taught them crying.
The years had weathered their complexions:
    too red at last for makeup,
    too blemished for photographers to hide.

Their children taught them crying
    and brought them far too much embarrassment
    to keep their perfect public reputations.
And thus they learned a need for God
    they only said they knew before.
And they grew real, yes, real, and yet again more real.

Then at last the growing melanoma came.
They fought the deep and hidden monster
    with huge machines that rumbled radiation.
And each day's loss reminded them
    that light is not forever, and the eye at last
    will be as hollow as the night.
And when the light is gone,
    it is far too dark to expect the world to stop and say,
    "Aren't they wise? Aren't they knowing?
    Let us learn from them
    As special teaching friends."

But wisdom moves so slow sometimes,
    when grief has amputated hope with darkness
    and crept upward from the numb and icy turf,
    cut like an earthen wound in winter snow.
They had buried their own hearts,
    interred their will to live.

But God does not allow his grace to slumber long.
There came to each a second Easter for their grief.
The tomb gave up its hopelessness.
The sealing stone rolled back; light shot through granite.
Then the day of visitation came.

Angels woke them both
    on an empty Saturday,
    somewhere near an ordinary market.
They met at last.
Each was dead of heart, dead of hope, alone.
    Her without him. Him without her.

"We haven't long to hold the light," he said.
"We haven't long," she said as she extended her hand,
    swollen with heavy knuckles that seemed unlovely
    even as she reached.
"She's gone; would she have minded?" he asked himself.
"Him, too. Would he have cared?" she wondered.
    They touch again.
Old hands do not play at passion.
    Eros is the cheap and hurried need of youth.
Their love was truly chaste now, too studied for impulsiveness,
    too knowing for rash need.
"I'll make you a salad," she said,
    ashamed her overtures for love were all so practical.
"My irises are in the second year," he said.
    He, too, could think of only small beginnings.

And, for the first time in heavy scores of months,
    two sets of footprints scrubbed the dewy grass
    because the years did not allow them
    to lift aging feet as high as they would like.
Those double footprints moved in one direction
    across the city park
    to the stoop of an old house
    still young enough to live a little while.

And sure enough,
　　the irises were all about the porch,
　　and inside, the silent lovers ate a crisp, fresh salad.
Their loneliness at last condensed itself into four slippers
　　set to dry upon a concrete stoop
　　that waited while naked feet
　　thrilled to feel the wet grass growing all about the irises.

The banners of their castle
　　waved proudly from a swagging laundry line—
　　one frayed and faded flannel shirt
　　and one bright gingham dress.
They wore them ever after—even on Memorial Day,
　　when they attended memories of other bargains
　　made with former lovers
　　in the springtime of their lives,
　　when their backs were straighter,
　　but their hearts were not made wise.

"She learned romance as she grew older."
Jane Austen, *Persuasion*

"Grow old along with me!
The best is yet to be,
The last of life, for which the first was made.
Our times are in his hand."
Robert Browning, *Rabbi Ben Ezra*

"A new command I give you: Love one another. As I have loved you,
so you must love one another."
John 13:34

"Better a meal of vegetables where there is love
than a fattened calf with hatred."
Proverbs 15:17

"He who finds a wife finds what is good
and receives favor from the LORD."
Proverbs 18:22

"Many waters cannot quench love; rivers cannot wash it away"
Song of Solomon 8:7

"For to be sure, he was crucified in weakness, yet he lives by God's power.
Likewise, we are weak in him, yet by God's power we will live with him to
serve you."
2 Corinthians 13:4